# WOODWORKING FROM THE SCRAP PILE

# WOODWORKING FROM THE SCRAP PILE

## 20 PROJECTS TO MAKE

DEREK JONES

The Taunton Press

The Taunton Press, Inc., 63 South Main Street
P.O. Box 5506, Newtown, CT 06470-5506
e-mail: tp@taunton.com

First published 2013 by
Guild of Master Craftsman Publications Ltd
Castle Place, 166 High Street, Lewes,
East Sussex BN7 1XU



Library of Congress Cataloging-in-Publication Data
Jones, Derek, 1964-
Woodworking from the scrap pile : 20 projects to make / Derek Jones.
pages cm
ISBN 978-1-62710-026-7 (paperback)
1. Woodwork. 2. Scrap materials. I. Title.
TT180.J66 2013
684'.08–dc23

2013029349



**Publisher** Jonathan Bailey
**Production Manager** Jim Bulley
**Managing Editor** Gerrie Purcell
**Senior Project Editor** Wendy McAngus
**Editor** Nicola Hodgson
**Managing Art Editor** Gilda Pacitti
**Design** Rob Janes and Chloë Alexander
**Photographs** Anthony Bailey and Derek Jones

Photograph at bottom of page 24 courtesy of Axminster Tool Centre Ltd.

Set in Futura
Color origination by GMC Reprographics
Printed and bound in China

10 9 8 7 6 5 4 3 2 1

**About Your Safety**

Working wood is inherently dangerous. Using hand or power tools improperly or ignoring safety practices can lead to permanent injury or even death. Don't try to perform operations you learn about here (or elsewhere) unless you're certain they are safe for you. If something about an operation doesn't feel right, don't do it. Enjoy the craft, but keep safety foremost in your mind whenever you're in the shop.

# CONTENTS

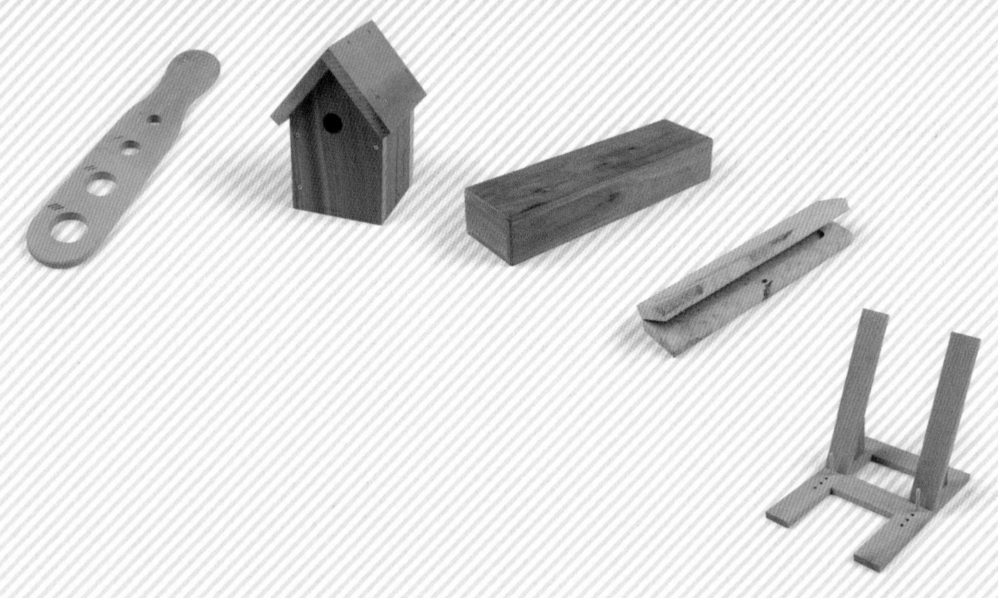



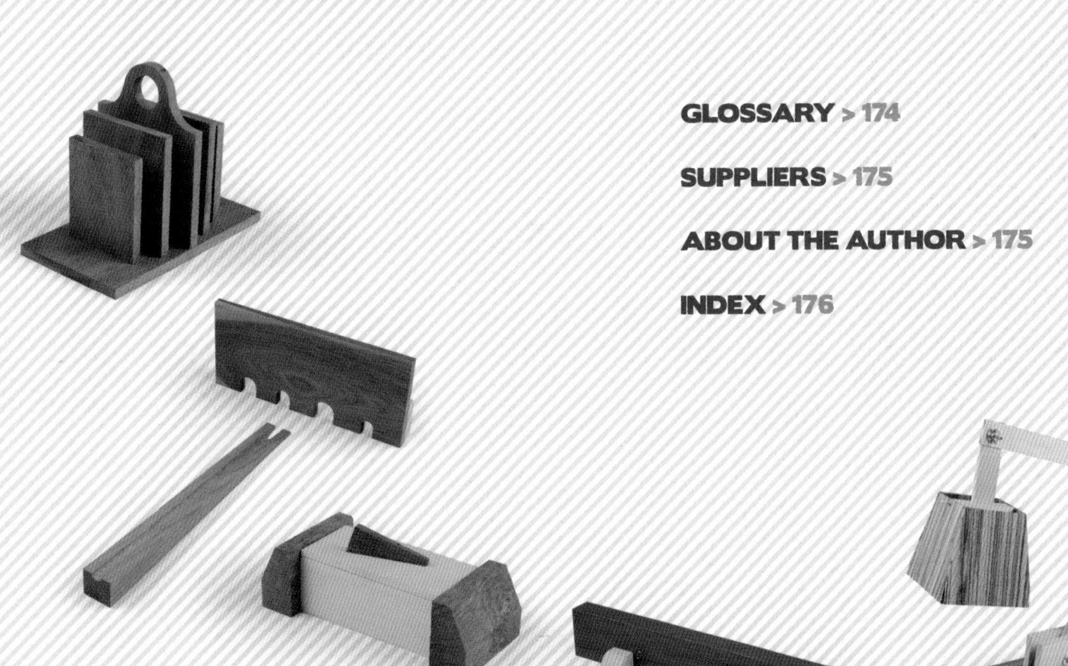

# INTRODUCTION

ONE PERSON'S SCRAP PILE IS ANOTHER PERSON'S PARTS LIST—OR AT LEAST THAT IS SOME OF THE REASONING BEHIND THIS BOOK.

I often think that we cherish our scrap pile a little too much, hoping that the perfect project will appear from nowhere and unleash a flurry of inspiration to make something useful out of that precious splinter of wood. It does happen, I know, but not that often. So, why not put an end to procrastination and turn that pile of wood to good use right away?

First, I can't imagine that anyone would want to make the projects contained within this book to save money when they can all be found in any good shop at a modest price. What I have in mind is something that money can't buy; not only will you get to keep the item forever, but you will also see a return on your investment like nothing else you've tried.

Rather than look at the projects as finished items, I want you to view them as a series of related techniques that build up into a comprehensive set of skills that will prepare you for more advanced work. There is no better way to learn a technique than within the framework of a real live project. As woodworking is a series of interdependent processes, it makes sense to learn these skills and see first-hand how they relate to each other and, more importantly, how you can adapt them to suit other applications.

For any project, the basis of the work is essentially a series of problems solved. With this book, I encourage you to look at everyday objects and ask yourself how you might go about making them, rather than how they were made. Your answer will depend on the equipment you have at your disposal and, just like your skills, this toolbox will undoubtedly grow as you develop ways to use them. In marketing terms, it's like pyramid selling. For the time being at least, think of these lessons as the first block on which to build something truly monumental.

*Derek Jones*

**NOTE ABOUT MEASUREMENTS**

All of the projects featured in this book were made from offcuts, and the emphasis is on the techniques and process required to make the projects. The measurements given are intended as a guide to give a sense of scale. You may need to adapt them according to the offcuts you are using and your preference for either metric or imperial systems.

My workshop uses the metric system and, because conversions to imperial can introduce inaccuracies, I recommend you stick to one measuring system or the other and cross-reference all multiples before generating your cutlist.

BOSCH
MARPLES
EZ Cal
FESTOOL

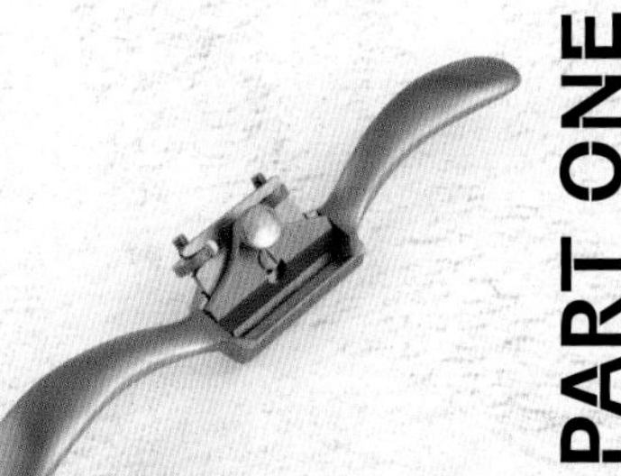

PART ONE

# BASICS

# TOOLS

## HAND TOOLS

### Marking and measuring tools

The first step, and therefore the most critical, in any project is that of capturing, generating, and transferring measurements. The most common measuring device is the tape measure. Although versatile, it is not suitable for making truly accurate measurements and should therefore be used solely for rough sizing. A pencil, no matter how sharp, falls into the same category; it should always give way to a more precise method of marking such as a knife or scalpel. A definite edge incised into the wood will give a clear indication of which side of the line to cut. A designated marking knife will have one completely flat side with which to register against a straight edge. The other side is ground with a bevel. These are often shaped to a point, making them suitable for working either left or right of the line.

A quality steel rule provides a convenient way to record measurements. It can be used in conjunction with a marking gauge to transfer marks to the workpiece. A sliding bevel is used to record and transfer angled measurements, sometimes from a protractor, while a square is used for lines of 90°. For absolute accuracy, nothing beats setting up a machine from a finished component or item of hardware. Where this is not feasible, a digital vernier caliper or digital angle gauge is the next best thing. For repeat marking of arcs, along with a host of other applications, a pair of dividers is invaluable.

**NOTE:** The measurements given in this book are intended only as a guide to give an idea of scale. You may need to adapt them according to the offcuts you are using. Stick to either imperial or metric measurements – don't mix them up.

*A dedicated marking knife is the most accurate means of scribing cut lines. The wedge-shaped line creates a positive reference for a chisel or saw blade.*

*A marking gauge or wheel gauge can be set to the required measurement for transferring onto the component.*

*Sliding bevels are used to record or transfer angles between components or machines.*

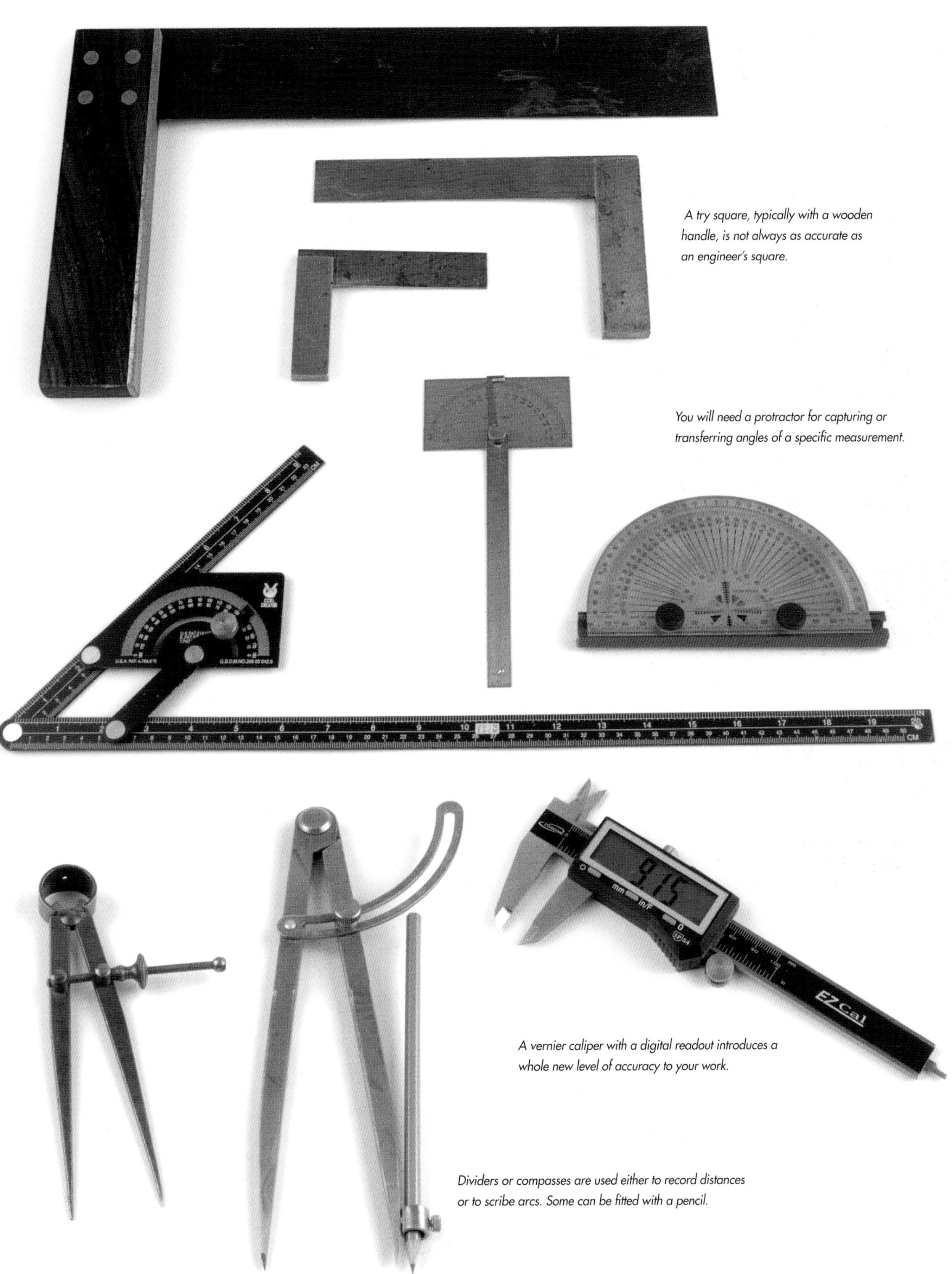


A try square, typically with a wooden handle, is not always as accurate as an engineer's square.

You will need a protractor for capturing or transferring angles of a specific measurement.

A vernier caliper with a digital readout introduces a whole new level of accuracy to your work.

Dividers or compasses are used either to record distances or to scribe arcs. Some can be fitted with a pencil.

### Saws

When it comes to saws, there are a few basics without which no toolkit can be considered complete.

Panel saws are primarily used to reduce sheet material into manageable sizes; these are available in a variety of tooth patterns to suit the material. When considering your purchase, bear in mind that a coarse tooth will generally cut more quickly, but it will require more work to remove the saw marks afterward.

Tenon and dovetail saws are designed specifically for cutting the joints that give them their name. These are available in different sizes to suit the scale of work and have a much finer tooth pattern. They are classed as "backed" saws; they are more commonly referred to as Western saws, as they feature a rigid strip of metal (typically brass) along the top edge of the blade.

Larger backed saws for use on carcase work, other than cutting mortise-and-tenons or dovetail joints, are sometimes available as either rip saws or crosscut saws. The terminology refers to their orientation in relation to the direction of the wood grain. A rip saw cuts with the grain; a crosscut saw cuts across the grain.

*Hardpoint panel saws, identified by their black or dark blue teeth, cannot be sharpened.*

*A tenon saw has a deeper blade to allow larger joints to be cut.*

*Gent's saws are convenient for fine work. Like these from Veritas, they are available with either a crosscut or rip saw tooth pattern.*

Japanese saws are unique in that they cut on the pull stroke rather than the push, as is the case with Western saws. The advantage is that the blade itself can be made of a much thinner material and with a typically finer set, or angle, to the teeth. The result is often a smoother finish and thinner kerf. The disadvantage is that once a cut has begun to wander, it is almost impossible to correct.

The teeth on a flush-cut saw have no set, meaning they do not protrude beyond the thickness of the blade. This allows you to trim flush with a surface without the risk of scratching it. Fret saws or coping saws are used to cut either tight curves or to gain access where a wider blade would not be suitable.

*Japanese saws have a flexible blade and are designed to work on the pull stroke.*

*Japanese saws come in a variety of tooth configurations and can be attached to a single handle.*

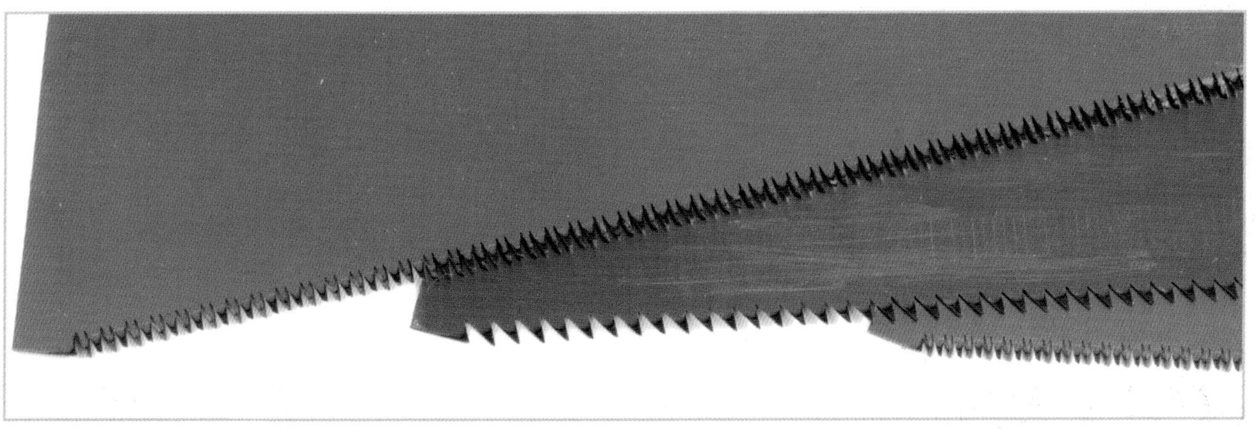

*A Japanese flush-cut saw has a very flexible blade, making it possible to trim dowels right up against the surface of a board.*

## Planes

For the majority of the projects in this book, you will require only two planes: a bench plane and a block plane. The ideal bench plane would be a No. 5; the ideal block plane would be a low-angled version for work on end grain. A cursory glance at any tool catalog will reveal numerous variants, all designed for specific uses. The benefits of owning these should relate to their intended use, as their features are not always suited to more than one task. For instance, a shoulder plane will allow you to work right up to an edge to create shoulders; a rabbet plane will enable you to produce rabbets without the use of a router or similar machine; and a plough plane will produce shoulders, rabbets, and grooves.

*Jointing or jack planes are used to flatten the edges of boards that are intended to be joined together. The wooden one from David Barron comes with a side fence to help maintain a square edge.*

*The larger shoulder plane with a fixed fine-mouth setting is a more specialized item; the smaller one, with an adjustable mouth, offers greater flexibility.*

*Two essential bench planes are the No. 5 and block plane.*

*The plough plane (far left) and the skew block plane (near left) can be used to produce rabbets or grooves.*

## Chisels

For the most part, chisels work in two ways: by slicing across the wood to produce thin shavings, or by driving straight through it in a chopping action. The cutting-edge geometry required for these separate functions is different. Therefore it is best to have chisels that are designed specifically for the job rather than making do with one set. A set of bench chisels ground to 25° with beveled sides will cover most workshop joinery and withstand a fair number of blows from a mallet when being used to cut joints such as dovetails. Paring chisels are generally ground with a 20° cutting edge and are used for finer work; they are not designed to be struck. Aside from the other specialized chisels, it may be useful to invest in one or two mortise chisels. These are made specifically for striking and are best used when paired with a matching-sized drill to produce mortises by hand.

Japanese chisels are becoming increasingly popular with Western woodworkers. In many respects, they perform just like Western chisels, having specific blades for particular applications. They require a slightly different approach to sharpening, but when mastered they are a joy to use.

*A good set of bevel-edge bench chisels from ¼ in. to 1 in. (6mm to 26mm) should cover most requirements.*

*Japanese chisels have the backs hollow-ground.*

*A selection of specialized chisels. Left to right: skew, mortise, and corner.*

*Some sort of protection is a good idea if you keep your chisels in a toolbox.*

## Hammers

Just like any other tool in the workshop, a hammer can do considerably more harm than good if it is not the right one. With this in mind, equip yourself with a selection of hammers and a mallet.

*This little brass chisel hammer from David Barron sits tight in the palm of your hand and helps to control the action of chopping out with a chisel.*

*Mallet, pin hammer, and Japanese hammer.*

## Screwdrivers

For all their convenience, I'm not a fan of screwdriver sets for anything other than general use. If you're fitting good-quality hardware or if you need to make fine adjustments, a dedicated screwdriver provides the most control over the task. When driving slotted screws, make sure the screwdriver tip is a good fit. Don't rule out having to grind one to size to fit older screw heads. Cross-head screws are generally Pozidriv, Phillips, or X-head; always use the appropriate driver for best results.

*It pays to have a wide selection of screwdrivers.*

### Clamps

You will often hear woodworkers say that you can never have too many clamps. This usually means that they have made something without considering how it will go together using the resources they have. Don't worry; we've all been there, but it pays to plan how you will assemble your work before you reach for the glue bottle. Clamps are also an important part of working safely to secure workpieces to the bench.

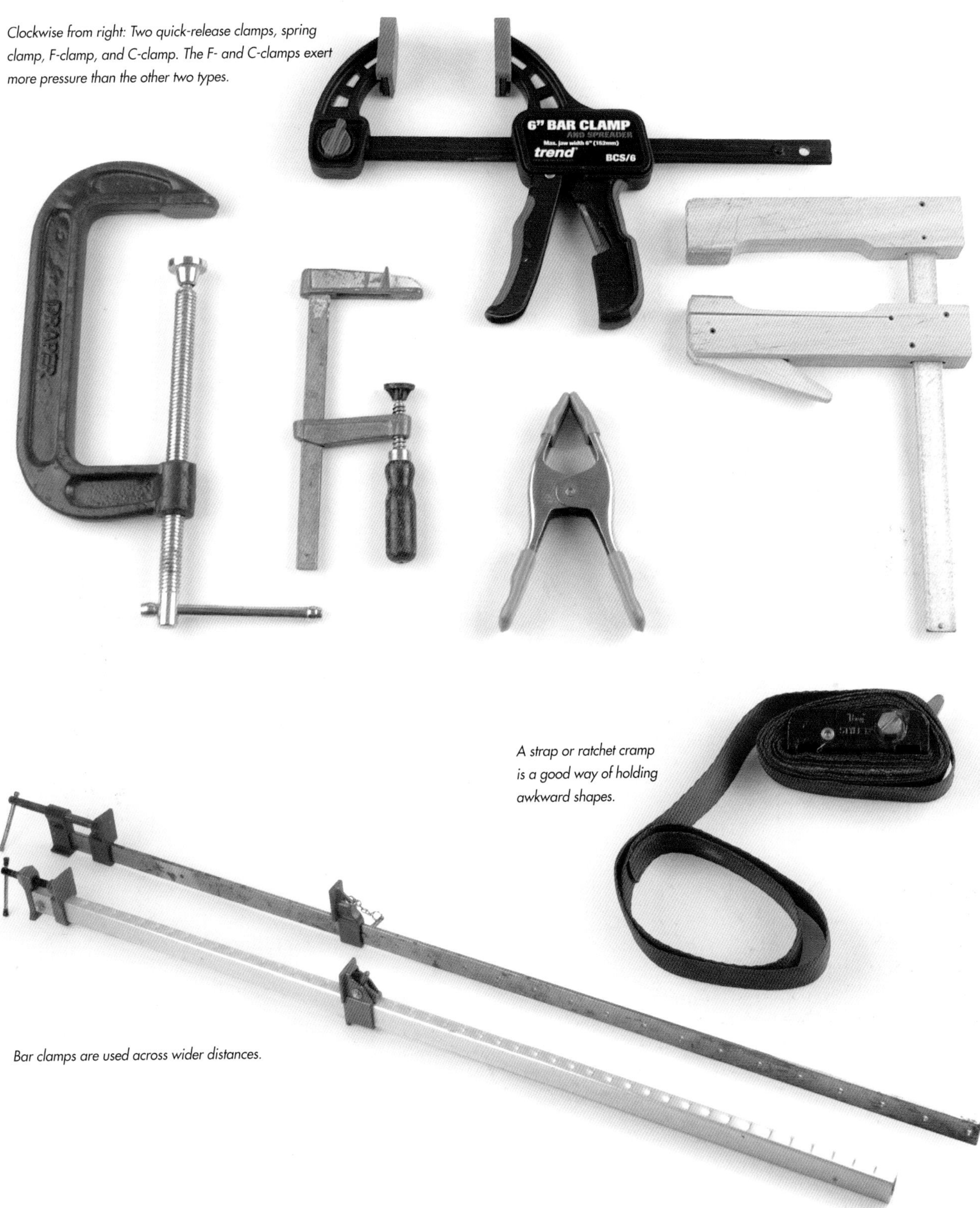


*Clockwise from right: Two quick-release clamps, spring clamp, F-clamp, and C-clamp. The F- and C-clamps exert more pressure than the other two types.*

*A strap or ratchet cramp is a good way of holding awkward shapes.*

*Bar clamps are used across wider distances.*

Rasps, preferably ones like these hand-stitched rasps from Workshop Heaven, will last for years.

## Shaping tools

Normal planes and chisels are ideal for flat work, but when creating shapes and curves, you will need a selection of tools perfectly suited to the task. This includes scrapers, rasps, and spokeshaves.

A spokeshave with fine blade adjustment is a good addition to your toolbox.

Cabinet scrapers come in all shapes and sizes. They can be used to smooth the surface of the wood.

## Sharpening tools

The sharpening and resharpening of tools is an inevitable consequence of working with wood. The subject has probably been discussed ever since people realized the advantages of having sharp-edged tools. Rather than turn this chapter into a treatise on sharpening, the best advice I can offer is to do it little and often with a system that you find easy to use. This might be a combination of water or diamond stones in conjunction with a honing guide or—my preferred method— a wet grinder and honing films (plastic sheets impregnated with fine abrasives).

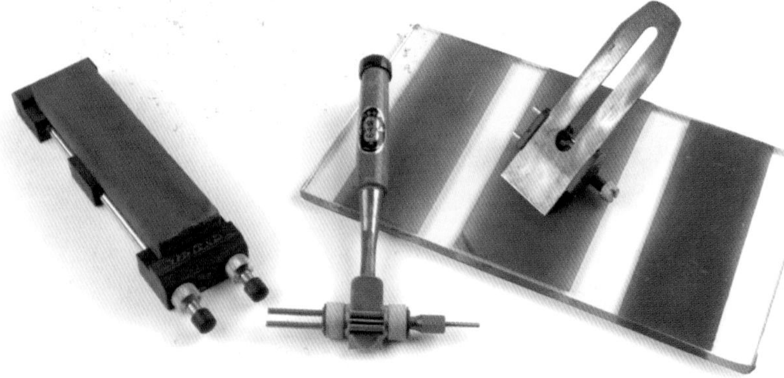

After grinding an edge on your chisel or plane blade it will require honing before you can say that it is truly sharp.

A dry grinding wheel will allow you to reshape tools or make your own, but will not achieve a truly sharp edge.

The Tormek wet grinder is perhaps the most versatile sharpening system available.

# POWER TOOLS

### Sanders

Not withstanding the noise and dust, electric sanders are a great addition to your power-tool lineup. A belt sander can be used to remove waste quickly and level off jointed boards. A random-orbit sander, depending on the size of its pad, can be used to flatten, shape, and finish wood prior to applying any finish.

*A random-orbit sander with the appropriate abrasive can be used to smooth wood without leaving a scratch pattern behind.*

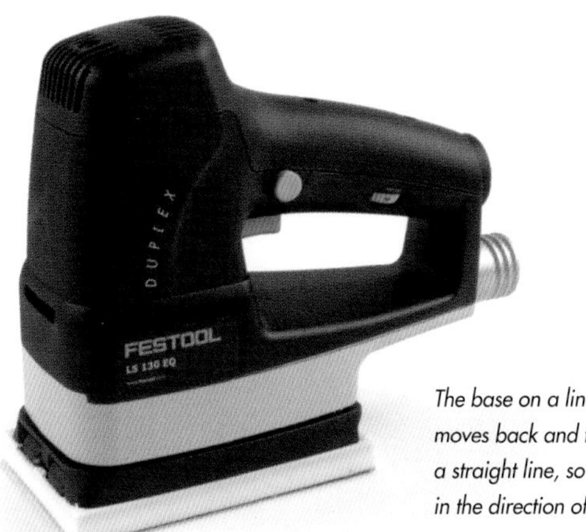


*The base on a linear sander moves back and forth in a straight line, so must be used in the direction of the grain.*

*Orbital sanders will leave behind a scratch pattern and are best used as preparation for a painted finish.*

*Belt sanders are designed for levelling surfaces before you do the finish sanding.*

### Jigsaws

For the most part, a jigsaw will do much the same job as a panel saw; it is often the most efficient means of reducing sheet material into manageable components. A jigsaw can also be used to fashion curves and irregular shapes and to cut holes in the middle of a board by first drilling a hole to insert the blade.

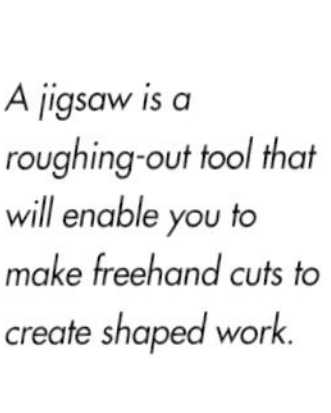


*A jigsaw is a roughing-out tool that will enable you to make freehand cuts to create shaped work.*

### Circular/Plunge saws

The integration of a guide-rail system with a circular saw has turned this once unruly tool into something more sophisticated. Circular and plunge saws are ideal for cutting boards and sheet material to dimension and for cutting bevels.

*A circular saw (right) is a good tool for reducing sheet material. A plunge saw (far right) can be used to start cuts in the middle of a sheet.*

### Biscuit jointer

A biscuit jointer is perhaps the most widely used means of creating machine-made joints in wood. It is quick to use and suitable for a number of applications, such as assembling and constructing carcases. It is an effective way to strengthen some joints, but is most useful as a way to connect mating components.

*A biscuit jointer is used to create semicircular grooves into which a lozenge-shaped spline is located.*

### Router

The router is a must-have for any serious woodworker. Using a variety of cutters, it will enable you to cut joints, add profiles to the edges of your work, and accurately trim components to size. For even more options, this tool can be mounted in a table, resulting in greater control and safer operation.

*Routers are typically available in two sizes: large and small. The larger will accept a wider range of cutters. Both machines can be used freehand or mounted in a table.*

### Cordless drill/driver

For any project that involves a lot of screws, a cordless driver will significantly cut down on the time spent assembling components. A cordless drill will have much the same effect. Rarely do combo tools provide the best of both worlds for cabinet work, so consider your requirements and choose accordingly.

*Cordless drills and drivers come in varying sizes to suit fine installation work and heavy-duty applications.*

# MACHINERY

A table saw will add a commercial feel to your working methods.

### Table saw

Often referred to as the heart of the workshop, a table saw can be used to reduce sheet goods and boards as well as cut pieces to exact size. A table saw requires specific blades to perform some tasks to get the full potential from your investment, but once acquired it will be with you for years.

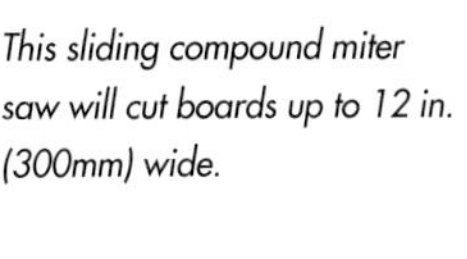

*This sliding compound miter saw will cut boards up to 12 in. (300mm) wide.*

### Miter saw

A miter saw, sometimes referred to as a chop saw, will allow you to make clean square cuts and miters. The more sophisticated machines will also tilt left and right to generate compound miters or bevel cuts. These are largely considered portable machines. If you don't own a table saw, a miter saw makes a welcome addition to the workshop.

### Jointer-planer

This machine will cut down on the amount of time spent squaring up wood and planing pieces to the required thickness. Floor-standing machines can be unwieldy beasts in a compact workshop, so consider a benchtop planer if you are not intending to work on large quantities of stock.

*A benchtop planer is more appropriate to a smaller shop but will require you to face and edge two of the four sides.*

*A combination jointer-planer will allow you to flatten all four faces of your stock in a fraction of the time it takes to do by hand.*

## Bandsaw

There are many woodworkers who say that a bandsaw is the only power saw you need. I'm not one of them, although I agree there is plenty you can achieve with a finely tuned machine and the right blade. Besides cutting shapes, a bandsaw can be used to cut thin sections from a thicker piece of stock more economically than using a table saw.

*A bandsaw's cut is limited by the distance from the blade to the body of the machine and the height of the guide wheels.*

## Benchtop sander

An oscillating spindle sander is a very useful machine for smoothing shaped pieces; with a little practice you can achieve quite consistent results. A disc sander, however, can perform with a greater degree of accuracy.

*An oscillating spindle sander will significantly speed up the process of smoothing the edges of curved work.*

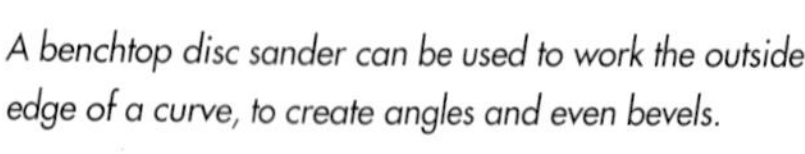

*A benchtop disc sander can be used to work the outside edge of a curve, to create angles and even bevels.*

## Drill press

In many instances, holes are drilled into wood to act as a point of alignment, so it makes sense to have a device that will do this accurately. There are benchtop versions and floor-mounted drill presses, and even drill stands that employ a hand drill.

*A portable drill guide (left) can be taken on site to drill holes accurately and freehand. A benchtop drill stand will take a portable drill.*

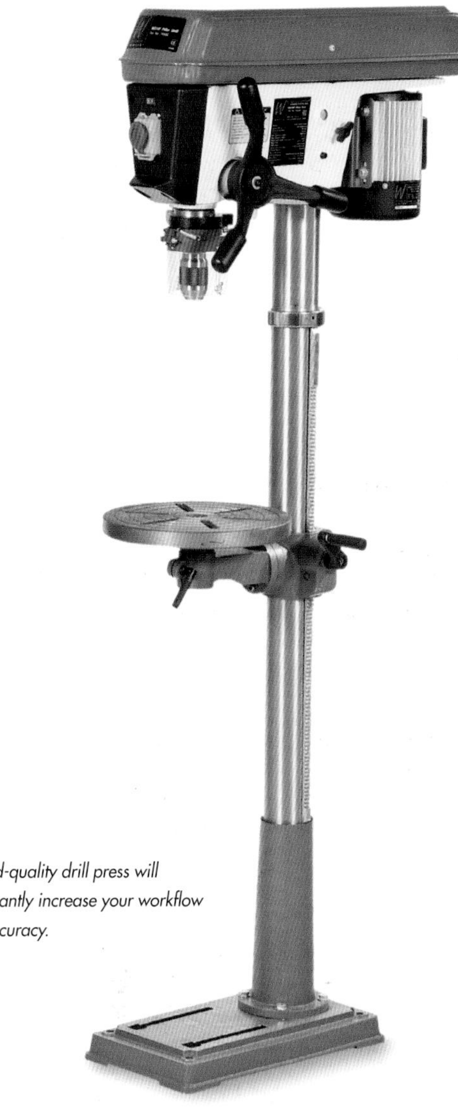

*A good-quality drill press will significantly increase your workflow and accuracy.*

## Accessories

There is virtually no end to the list of accessories available to the woodworker. As with most things in life, you get what you pay for. Saw blades and drill bits can be sharpened, so these represent a significant investment if you want them to last and perform well. Other consumables, such as bandsaw blades and router bits, are either difficult or impractical to maintain for any length of time, so can be regarded as disposable.

*Every machine requires tooling of some sort; it pays to buy the best quality you can.*

# MATERIALS AND JIGS

## MATERIALS

**What offcuts to save**

The chances are that during the course of your woodworking lifetime you'll turn more filler into dust than what remains on the job. Fortunately, the odds are slightly more in your favor when it comes to wood. But with so much material passing through the workshop, what is worth saving and what is not? For a start, anything with a fault, such as splits or knots, can be passed over as unsuitable for any large-scale project. Longer lengths that display signs of severe movement, such as twists or bows, are likely to require considerable effort to convert them into workable material. They are probably not worthwhile—but make an exception for exotic species or smaller sections that might work well as a contrasting detail like a handle or an inlay.

It is easy to get into the habit of hoarding beyond what is a realistic level of stock; I work on the principle that if the material was good enough to make furniture from in the first place, the offcuts will be acceptable for anything that follows. With regard to size, your selection process might be dictated by what equipment you have. Any pieces that are too small to pass through a machine safely (if that is your preferred method of working) can be disposed of.

Batch production can yield a quantity of uniform offcuts that might otherwise be costly to produce; many commercial workshops look for opportunities to convert these into products for sale. As tempting as it is, I remain unconvinced of the benefits of this practice for smaller workshops without an existing route to market that can be piggy-backed. Your time might also be better spent squaring off random-shaped offcuts as sheet material for more efficient storage instead.

**What offcuts to avoid**

There is a huge demand for reclaimed wood. The commercially harvested product is generally quite acceptable, but beware of wood-based products that have not been used for quality work the first time around. Packing materials are especially unsuitable because the wood will be of poor quality and unlikely to have been seasoned. It can also contain foreign bodies such as staples and nails.

**How to store offcuts**

Space is likely to be your primary concern. If you are serious about using offcuts, store them as you would your main stock —in dry conditions, preferably in racks where they cannot develop faults. Depending on the scale of your operation you may wish to separate offcuts by species or at least separate manmade products and solid wood.

**A source of inspiration**

The individual characteristics of a piece of wood can be all the inspiration you need to develop a design for something unique, so look out for such opportunities. The end of a board with some wild grain might not have been suitable for a set of stiles and rails for a door, but it might sing out to you as a decorative panel within a frame. The most famous exponent of this style is perhaps George Nakashima; he made splits and naturally occurring faults in the wood an integral part of his work, often embellishing the details with additional features.

**Where to find free offcuts**

A growing number of commercial workshops are moving toward recycling offcuts to produce fuel for heating. However, it is still possible to find a cabinetmaker in your area who is willing to part with a bag of sizeable blocks for a modest fee or even for free.

## JIGS

A common feature in any established woodworking shop will be a collection of jigs and templates. These handmade devices are used to simplify some of the more repetitive processes and make others a great deal safer. Templates, if well made and stored properly, can be used repeatedly to generate duplicate components on the same project or again years later. Jigs, on the other hand, can be used every day to introduce accuracy and convenience to almost any task. Here I give you three jigs to start off with; they are all used in this book and hopefully will inspire you to create some of your own.

## Box alignment jig

Whenever you are working with thin material, any inaccuracies with either the cutting or marking are hard to absorb into the process. Add to this the fragile nature of the finished object and you begin to realize why it can take nearly as much time to make an intricate jewelry box as it does a full-size wardrobe. The answer to most problems in the workshop is to make a jig that helps you avoid having to do things more than once and to unify some parts of the construction. An alignment jig is a perfect solution for drilling accurate holes in mating components without having to mark them twice. It can also be used to hold components in position while laying out the joints. The only critical factor is that it is square at one corner. The dimensions are up to you.

**Plan**

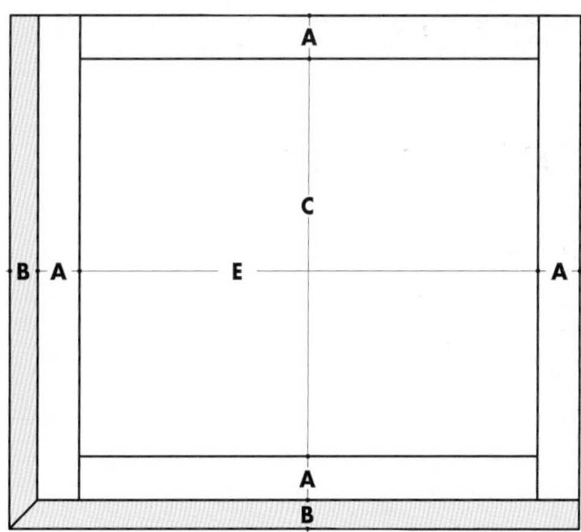


**KEY**
**A = ¾ in. (19mm)**
**B = ½ in. (12mm)**
**C = 6 ½ in. (165mm)**
**D = 4 ¾ in. (121mm)**
**E = 7 ¾ in. (197mm)**

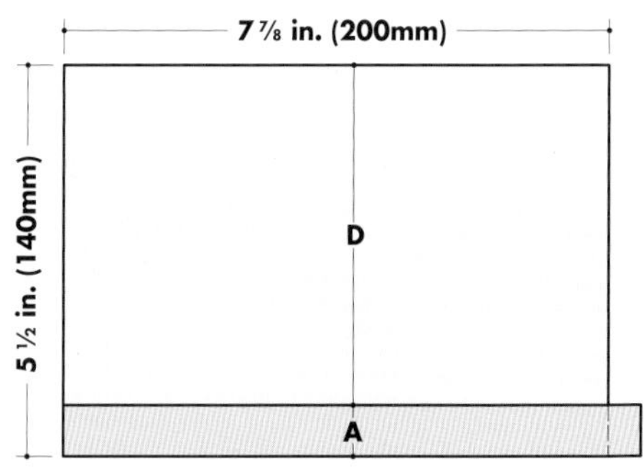


**Side Elevation**

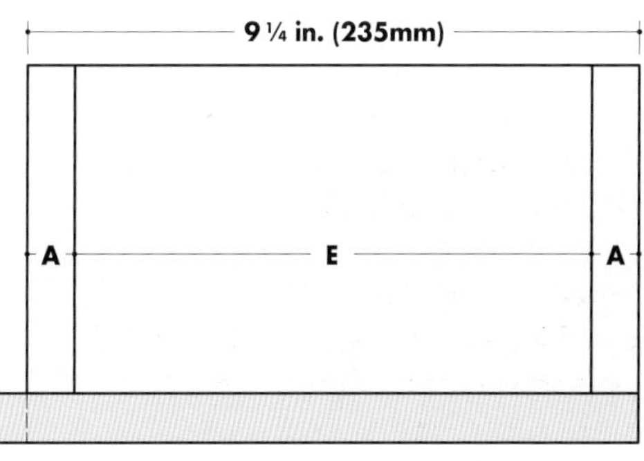


**Front Elevation**

**1** Select the material for your box and prepare the components so that they are straight and square on all edges. Mark them out for your chosen method of construction and indicate how they relate to each other.

**2** I used birch plywood to make my box and biscuits to assemble it, although screws would also be quite acceptable. For a box this size (approximately 8 in./200mm square), a single biscuit at each corner is adequate. By clamping a board to the bench you have created your first jig: it provides a stable edge to work against.

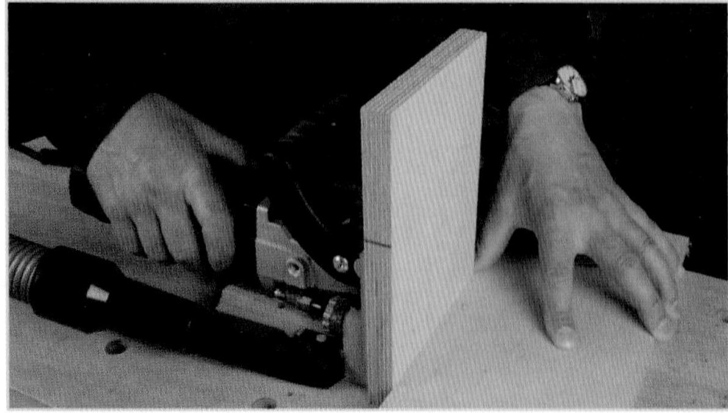

**3** Biscuit jointers are quick to use because they require minimal marking of the joints. The board allows you to work efficiently without the need to keep moving clamps.

**4** In theory, if all your edges were square, the box should go together square, but always check by measuring from corner to corner in two directions. The dimensions should be exactly the same.

**5** When you are satisfied with the box, select the best corner to plant a small fence along two edges with mitered corners.

**6** You can ignore the outside edge of the box and focus on making sure that the inside faces of the two fences are square with the corner edge of the box and are therefore in line.

**7** Tack and glue the fences in place.

**8** The finished box alignment jig. Now see how this can be put into use in the Letter Rack project on pages 124–129.

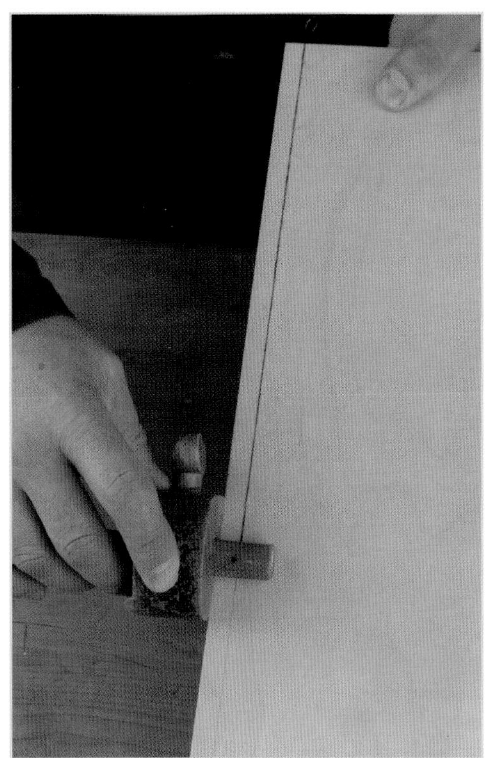

### Bench hook

A bench hook is essentially a cutting surface with a back stop or fence in place to support small sections of wood for cutting freehand with a saw. There is no need to clamp it in place; the action of sawing will prevent it from moving—just place it down where it is needed and you are ready to start cutting. The base is a sacrificial component that will prevent you from creating a saw cut in your benchtop. I have found it useful to have one that I can use with either Western or Japanese saws.

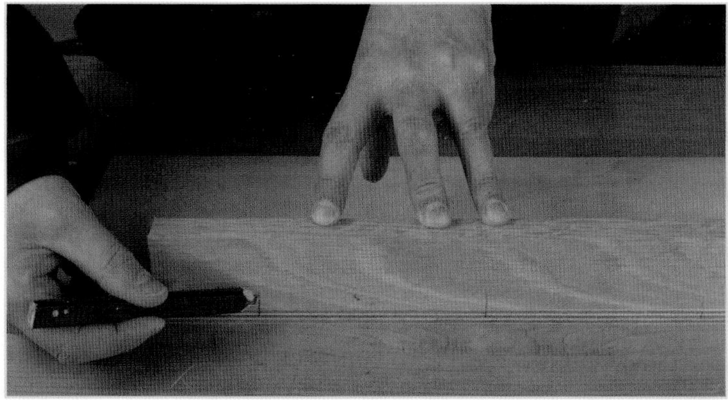

**1** With any flat piece of board—MDF or ply will do—mark a center line along one long edge in preparation for screwing a fence to the other face flush with the edge of the board. Then mark the middle of the board at the edge to indicate the position of the first screw.

**2** Find the middle of the fence and hold it in place against the center mark on the baseboard. By eye, place marks on either side of the center for two more screws. The measurements are not critical, but if you keep the screws a good 2 in. (50mm) away from the end, you will be able to trim the jig later when it shows signs of wear and tear. Note that the fence is also a fair bit shorter than the baseboard.

**3** Before drilling the holes for the screws, mark a second row on the opposite side of the baseboard about 2 in. (50mm) away from the back edge. This will be the position for the second fence or hook, depending which way round you want to use it.

**4** Drill all the holes to suit the screws and countersink them if necessary.

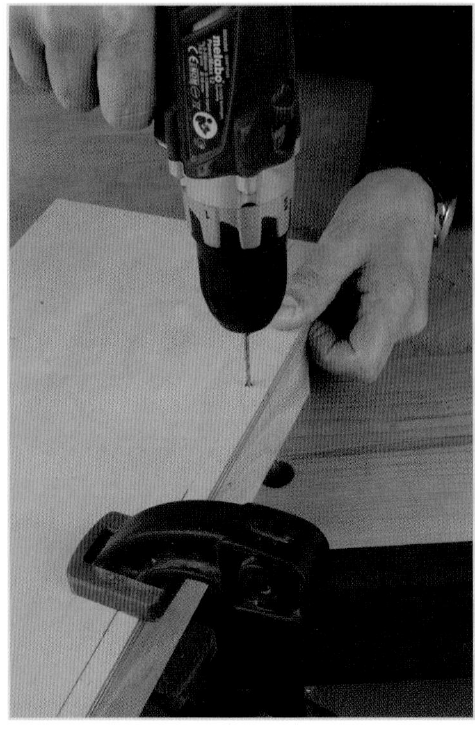

5 Clamp the fence components in place, drill pilot holes, and screw them in place.

6 By now it should be obvious where this jig gets its name, as either fence can be used to hook over the benchtop.

7 With the hook this way up, you can use it with Western saws.

8 The other way up is perfect for using with Japanese saws. Providing you haven't used glue to attach the fences, they can be removed, trimmed, or just relocated along the center line to keep the jig in tip-top condition.

## Shooting board

The shooting board performs a similar function to the bench hook but is used with a plane, preferably a long one. It is a device that holds a piece of wood to be shaped to a level of accuracy that would prove difficult to achieve free-hand. Its primary function is to assist with planing the end of stock, which is typically end grain. The material is pushed tight up against a back fence set at 90° to a runway used to guide the plane squarely across the end of the stock. With a sharp blade it is possible to trim the finest of shavings. The accuracy of your shooting board will depend on flat, level surfaces and clean, square edges to all the components. Good-quality ply or moisture-resistant MDF are the best materials to use.

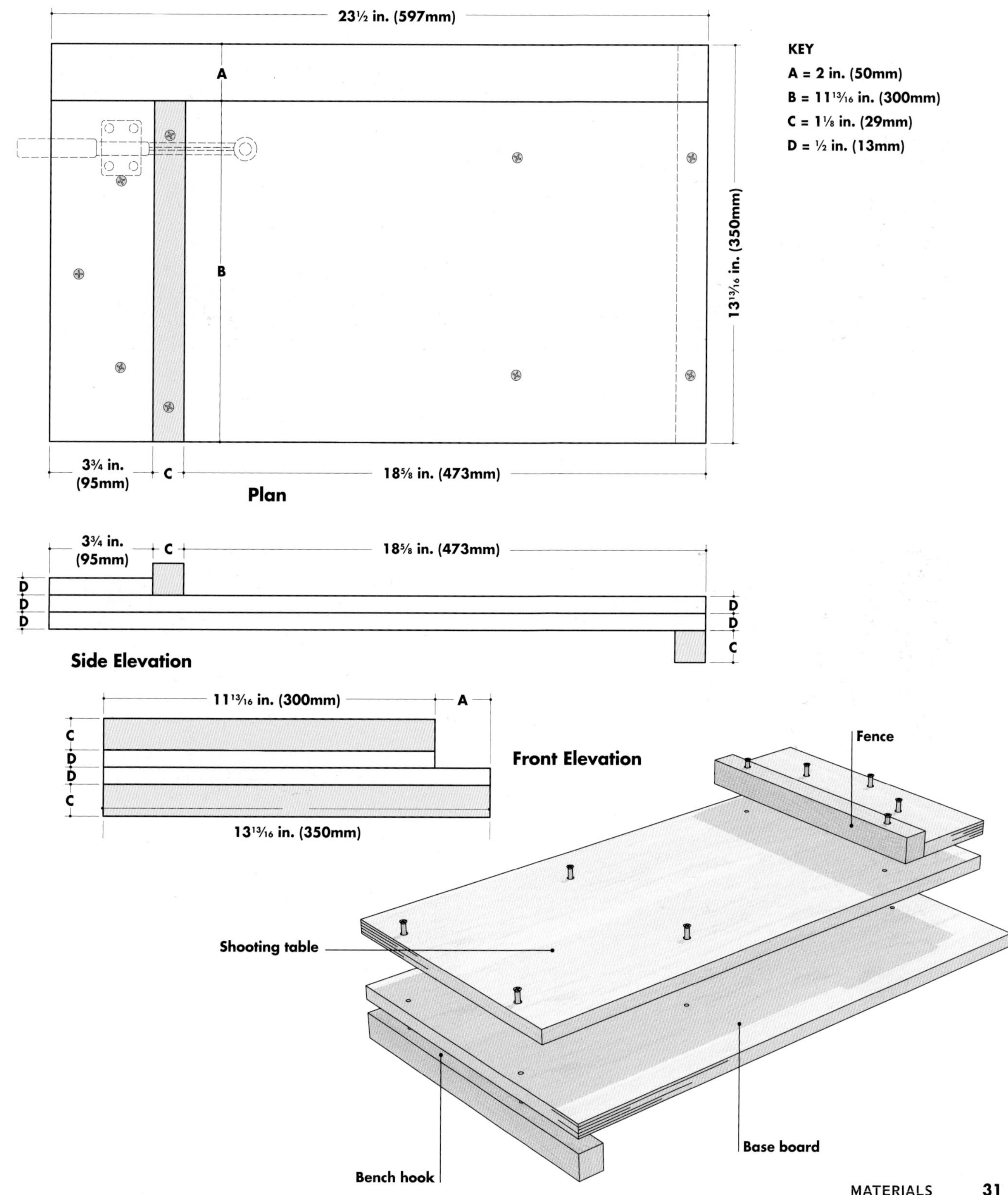

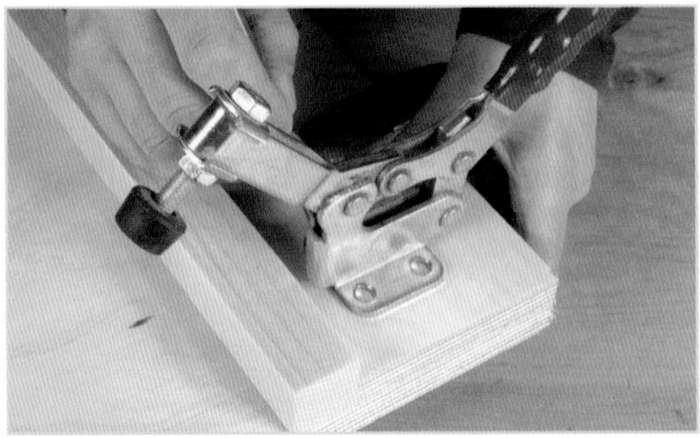

1 The first and most important task is to plant the back stop onto the main table perfectly square to one edge, to the right if you are right-handed.

2 A second fence will sit against the back stop, over which you can fit a toggle clamp. Check the location of these components and mark out for the hardware.

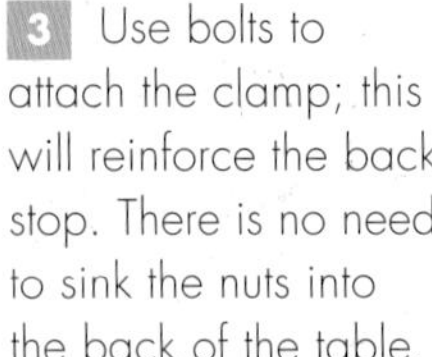

3 Use bolts to attach the clamp; this will reinforce the back stop. There is no need to sink the nuts into the back of the table.

4 Instead, mark their location on the top of the baseboard and bore over-sized holes to accommodate them.

5 Plant the main tabletop onto the baseboard and attach it with screws. Use a countersink to make sure the heads lie below the surface. At the front end, attach a hook to the underside so the jig can be braced against the edge of the bench.

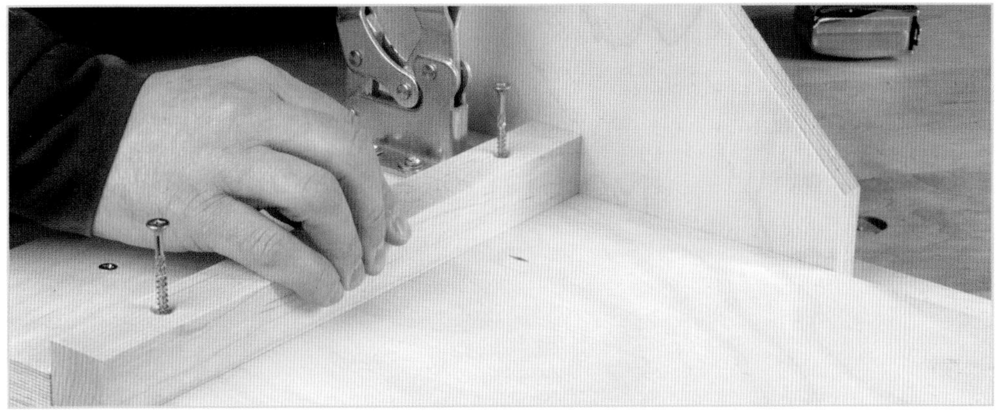

**6** Mount the fence onto the main table, making sure it is flush with the right-hand edge of the main table. A suitable block of wood will help. Drill the pilot holes through the fence for the screws $\frac{1}{64}$ in. (0.5mm) over-size.

**7** Slip paper as a shim behind the fence to obtain a perfectly square fence in relation to the right-hand edge of the main table.

**8** You may now want to remove some of the sharp edges so the jig is a pleasure to use.

**9** With a suitable bench plane on its side you can now glide it along the runway to shoot the ends of stock square and to dimension.

**10** Use supports like this one cut at 45° to shoot angles.

PART TWO

# PROJECTS

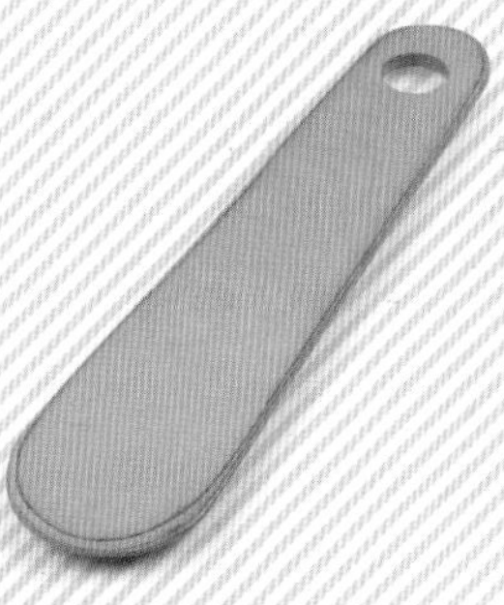

# SERVING PLATTER

I chose this to be the first project in the book to illustrate what you can make in less than 30 minutes with scraps that might otherwise have been thrown away. Birch plywood is a high-quality material, so it pays to use up every last bit of it. This platter is ideal for serving baguettes or garlic bread.

There is nothing technically challenging here in terms of construction, but don't be fooled: rounding over edges to a uniform profile requires a good eye. Belt sanders are generally considered coarse machines, but they also have a gentle side if you know where to find it.

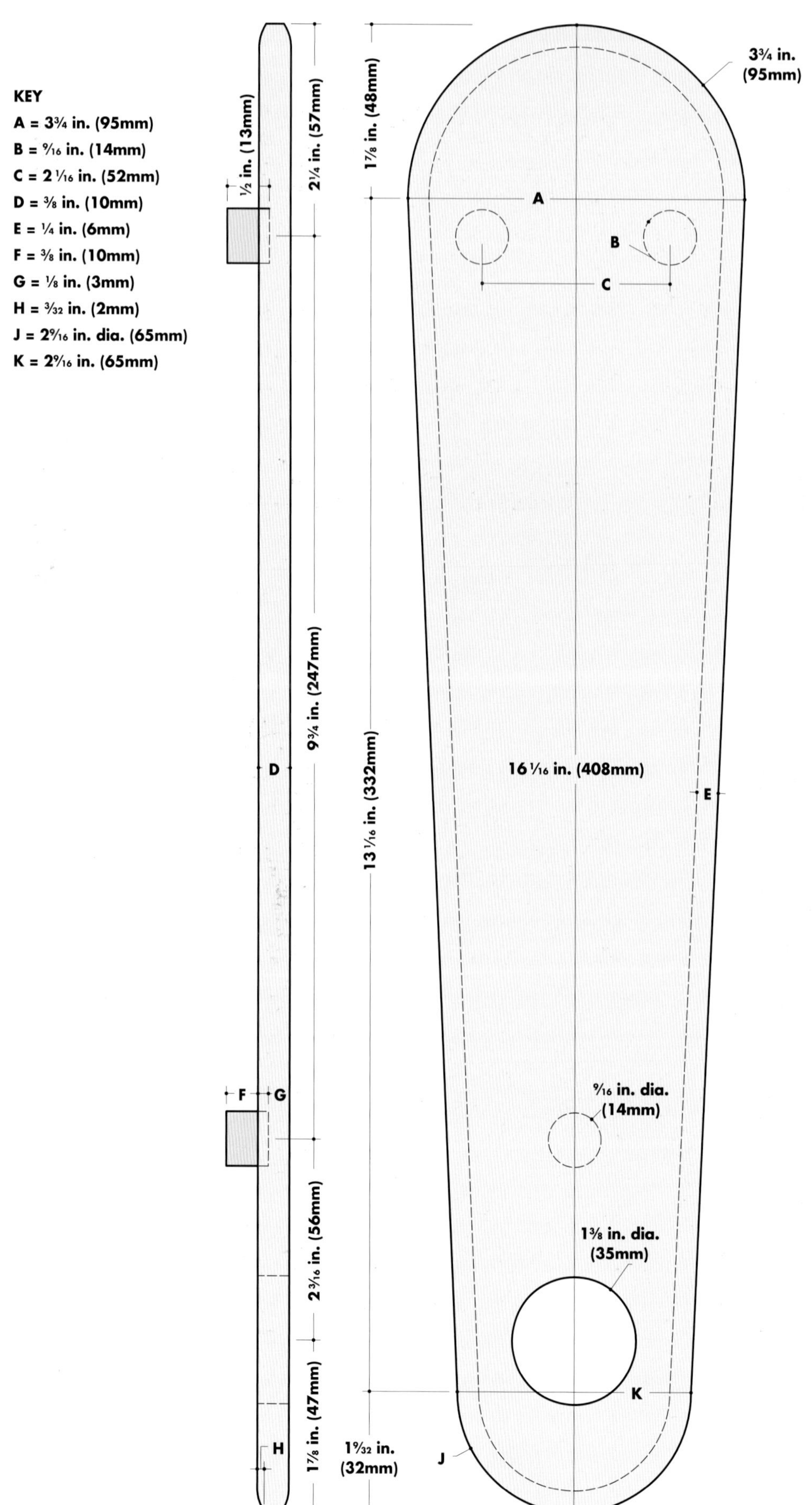
KEY
A = 3¾ in. (95mm)
B = 9/16 in. (14mm)
C = 2 1/16 in. (52mm)
D = 3/8 in. (10mm)
E = 1/4 in. (6mm)
F = 3/8 in. (10mm)
G = 1/8 in. (3mm)
H = 3/32 in. (2mm)
J = 2 9/16 in. dia. (65mm)
K = 2 9/16 in. (65mm)
1/2 in. (13mm)
2¼ in. (57mm)
1 7/8 in. (48mm)
3¾ in. (95mm)
A
B
C
9¾ in. (247mm)
13 1/16 in. (332mm)
16 1/16 in. (408mm)
D
E
F
G
9/16 in. dia. (14mm)
1 3/8 in. dia. (35mm)
2 3/16 in. (56mm)
1 7/8 in. (47mm)
H
1 9/32 in. (32mm)
J
K

1 Mark out the shape of your platter on one board and draw a center line down the middle of both to position the curves and through-hole.

2 While the boards are still square, draw a couple of lines square to the edge from one side.

3 Cut one platter to shape on the bandsaw and use it as a template to shape the second.

**4** Use an upturned belt sander to shape the radius on the ends of the boards. Keep the board angled back from the direction of the belt and never work beyond a vertical position. Apply gentle pressure and keep the board moving at all times.

**5** Using the same principle, start to work on the edges by rolling around the radius at both ends. Use the layers of the ply to achieve a uniform bevel around the curve.

**6** Continue the bevel down the long sides; maintain an even line by using the colors of the plies as a guide.

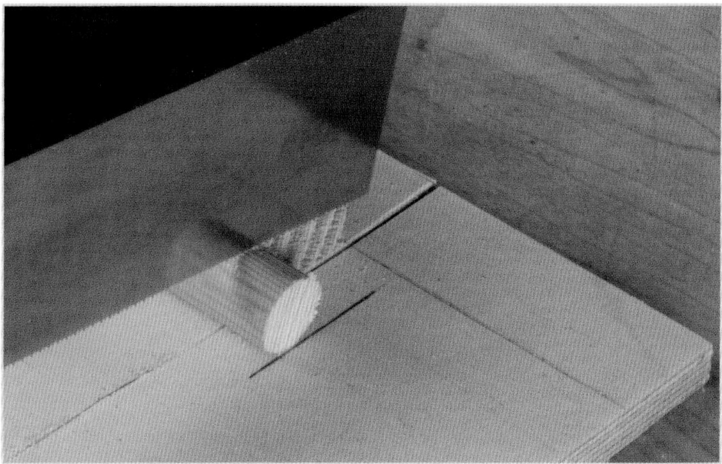

7 Cut short lengths of dowel to be used as feet and drill suitably sized blind holes along the lines that come in from the side.

8 Sand off all the pencil marks and glue the feet in place.

*Your finished serving platter will look something like this.*

# MARBLE GAME

This project – to make a game that tests your ability to roll a marble down the ramp and through one of the holes – introduces some very basic techniques for marking out and cutting to a line when dealing with circles and angles. It will help you to identify why it is important to establish which side of the line to make your cut. We will use a marking knife for the most critical lines.

Offcuts can also be used in the making of a project, especially when working with curved or angled pieces like the ramp in this one.

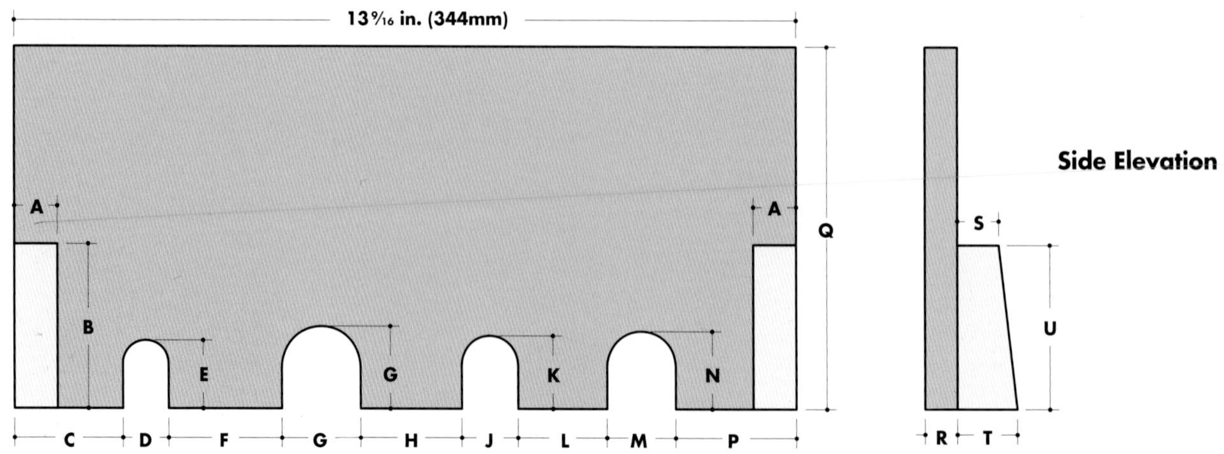


**Front Elevation**

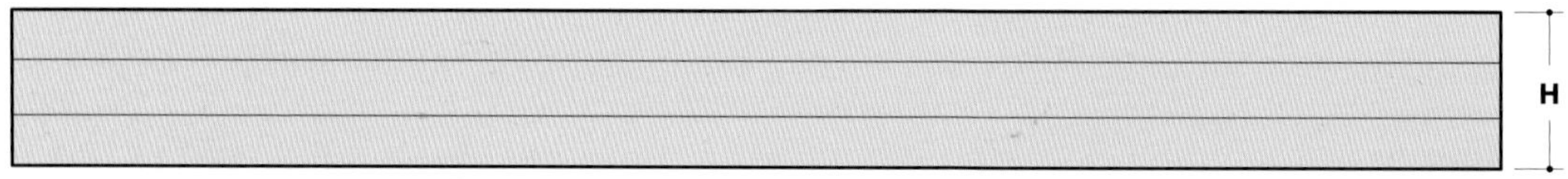

V
W
X
W
17 ½ in. (444mm)
H
H

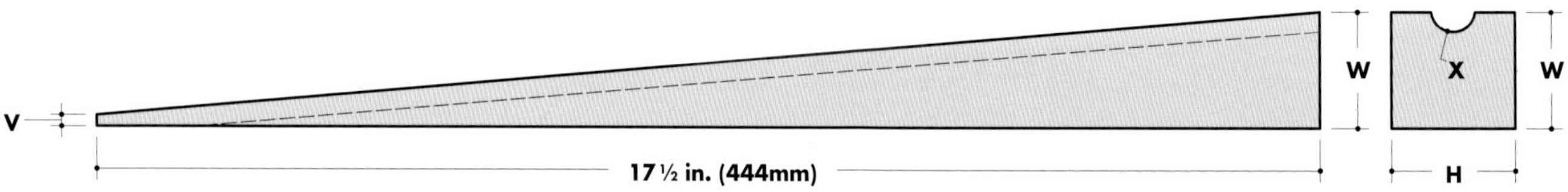

**Plan**

**KEY**

A = ¾ in. (19mm)
B = 2¾ in. (70mm)
C = 1⅞ in. (48mm)
D = ¾ in. (19mm)
E = 1⅛ in. (29mm)
F = 2 in. (51mm)
G = 1⅜ in. (35mm)
H = 1¾ in. (44mm)
J = 1 in. (25mm)
K = 1¼ in. (32mm)
L = 1 9/16 in. (40mm)
M = 1 3/16 in. (30mm)
N = 1¼ in. (32mm)
P = 2 1/16 in. (52mm)
Q = 6 in. (152mm)
R = ½ in. (12mm)
S = ⅝ in. (16mm)
T = 1 in. (25mm)
U = 2¾ in. (70mm)
V = ⅛ in. (3mm)
W = 1⅝ in. (41mm)
X = ⅝ in. dia. (16mm)

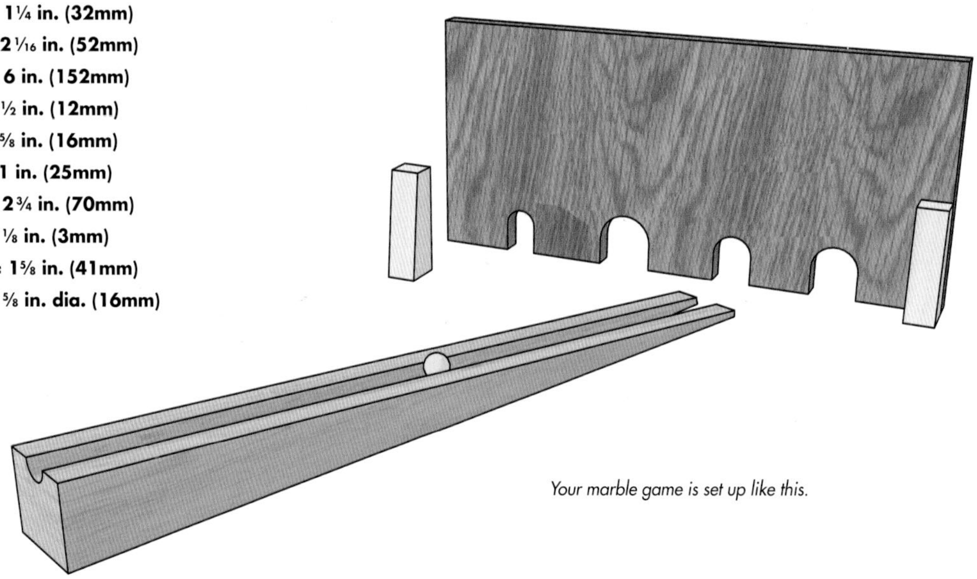

*Your marble game is set up like this.*

1 Create a channel down the middle of a squared-up piece of stock to suit the size of your marbles.

2 Cut the wedge shape on the bandsaw to produce the ramp. Retain the offcut. Place the ramp, sawn face up, on the back of the offcut and place the two pieces in a vise. Now plane the ramp using the offcut to support the thin edge of the wedge.

3 Remove the ends of the wedge with a handsaw.

4 Using an assortment of drill bits, set a marking gauge to the radius of the largest bit.

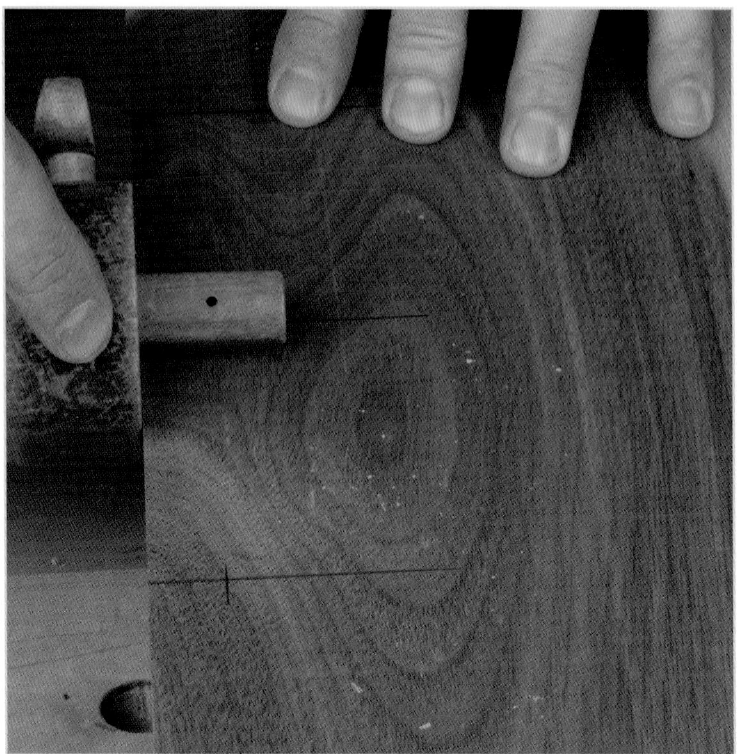

5 Mark this measurement along lines marked at regular intervals on the face of the goal.

6 Drill the holes and, using a marking knife, mark lines from the edge of the circles to the edge of the board. Make sure the lines correspond with the edge of the hole.

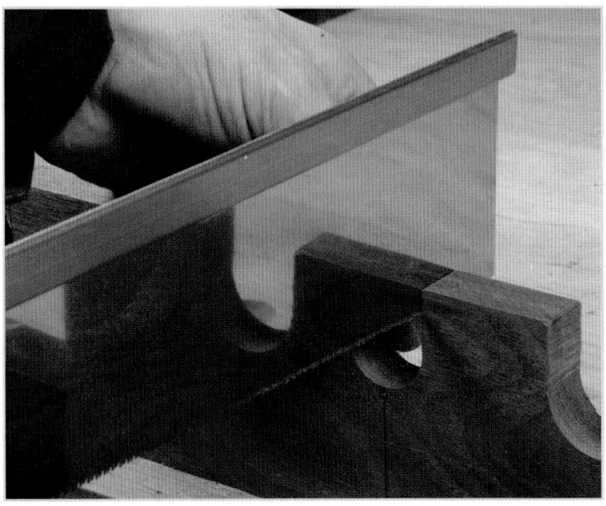

7 Using a handsaw, cut on the side of the knife mark that will result in the blade entering the hole and not passing alongside it.

8 Finally, glue a couple of supports to the back of the goal and add some numbers to the front.

*Your finished marble game will look something like this.*

# RING BOX

If you have made your bench hook and shooting board (see pages 29–33), you are already halfway there with this project. This is a perfect way to hone your sawing, marking, and trimming techniques on small components as well as to use up precious offcuts of exotic wood and veneer. The proportions need not be square and, although this project is presented as a ring box, it could be adapted to store larger items.

The key to success with this project is to make sure your stock is planed flat and square on all four faces, so pay attention to which side of the line you are working to. There are 24 mating edges on this cube, all of which are visible, so cut oversize and trim to fit to achieve the best results.

**KEY**

A = ⅜ in. (10mm)
B = 1⅜ in. (35mm)
C = 1/32 in. (1mm)
D = ⅛ in. (3mm)
E = 3/16 in. (5mm)
F = ¼ in. (6mm)
G = 1 1/16 in. (27mm)
H = 1 in. (25mm)
J = 1¾ in. (44mm)

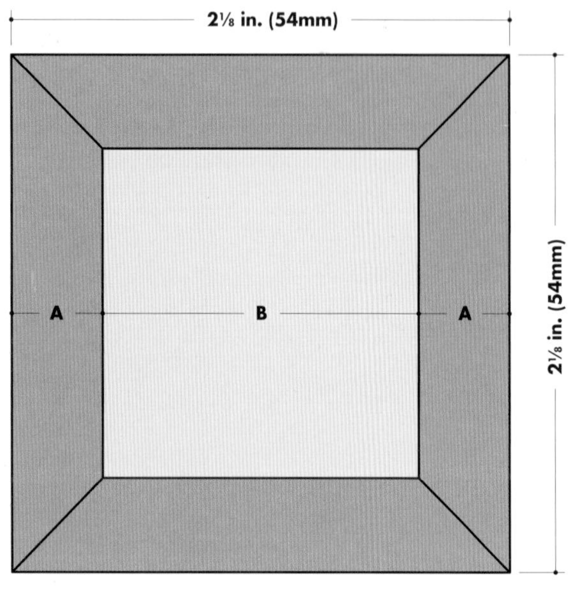


Plan

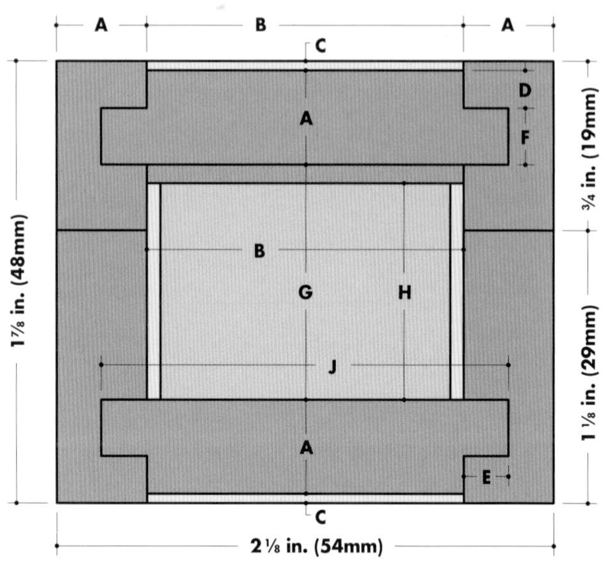


Section

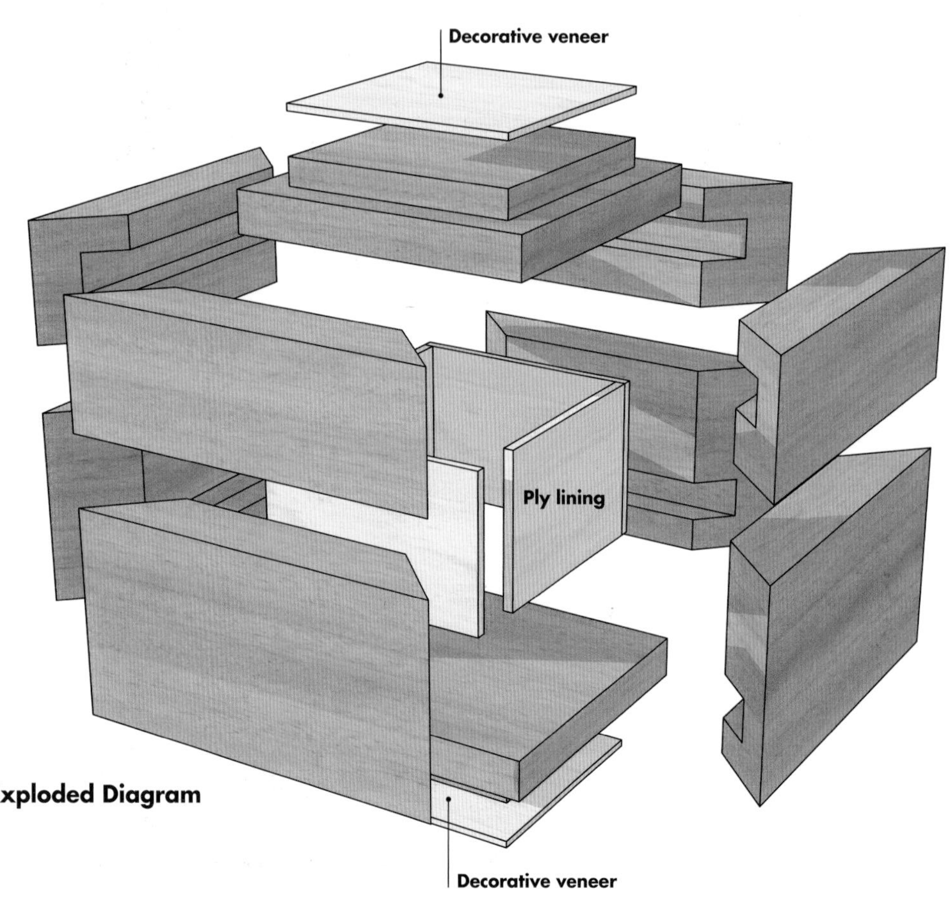


Exploded Diagram

**1** Select your offcuts; I used lengths of purpleheart and some bird's eye maple veneer for this project, cutting the veneer slightly wider than the purpleheart.

**2** Apply a thin coat of glue to one face of the solid wood (not veneer). Spread the glue evenly across the whole width of the board.

**3** Sandwich the solid wood and veneer together using one of the solid 2⅛-in. (54mm) boards as a press. Apply pressure with clamps evenly across the stack.

4 Cut a rabbet on two edges of the veneered face and a corresponding groove along two edges of the plain board. Try to achieve a reasonably tight fit, with the veneered surface set slightly lower than the edge of the board.

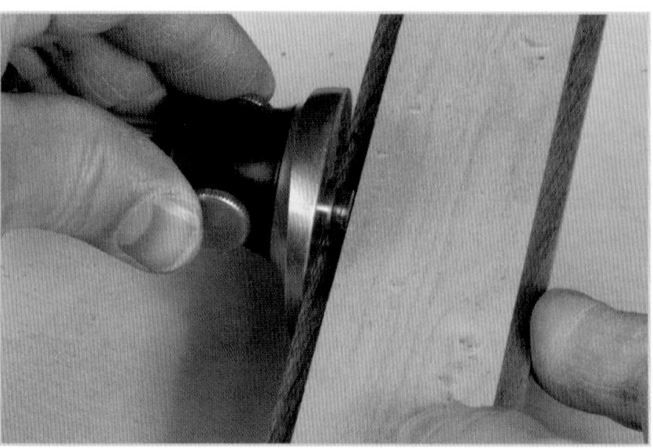

5 Cut and trim a square edge on the veneered board and set a marking gauge to the width of the rabbet.

6 Transfer this measurement to the end and cut the shoulder to form a full-width tenon.

7 Use a shoulder plane to trim the tenon to size.

8 Mark for the shoulder on the other end, remembering to cut on the correct side of the line.

**9** Use the first component to measure out for the second. The most important edge is the shoulder line, not the overall dimension, which can be reduced to fit later.

**10** Label the mating component edges before marking the corner miters.

**11** Cut miters oversize with the aid of a miter block clamped to your bench hook.

**12** Trim the miters with a low-angle block plane on the shooting board with a mitered support block in front and behind the workpiece.

**13** If you undercut any of the miters, you can adjust the shoulder lines of the insert, but remember to alter the top and the bottom. You might find it easier to glue the box up in two halves.

14 Use a cabinet scraper to trim the top and bottom edges of the box to the veneer.

15 Use a marking gauge to strike a line where you want the lid of the box.

16 To avoid a mistake, cut on the line to split the box by first making cuts part-way through the sides to establish a continuous saw line.

17 Level the edges using a sheet of sandpaper stuck to a flat board. Work from corner to corner, a couple of strokes at a time, and then rotate.

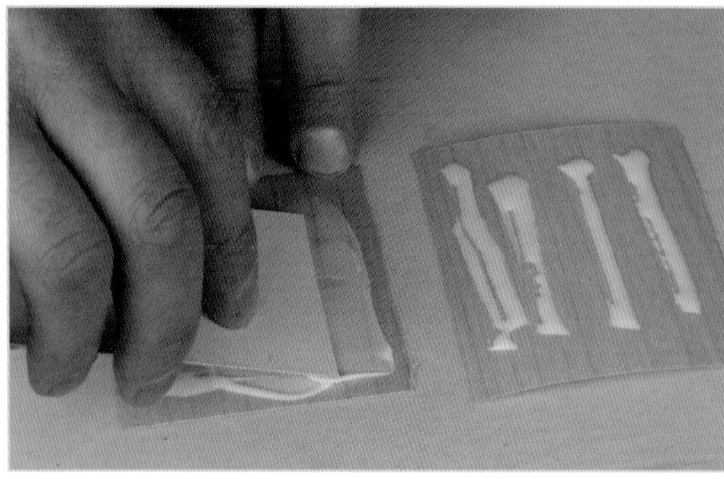

18 Make up some thin ply with three strips of veneer. Lay one piece with the grain opposing the direction of the outer layer.

**19** Cut the inserts oversize and trim them to fit on the shooting board.

**20** Glue the inserts in place one at a time.

*Your finished ring box will look something like this.*

# PICTURE FRAME

At first glance, a picture frame seems fairly straightforward to make. The eight identical miters are generally considered to be the most difficult aspect to master. But when made out of solid section, the complexity of the item shifts to a feature that will never see the light of day and, if not executed accurately, will make perfect miters virtually impossible.

Whether you use a shaper or a router to produce rabbets, the problem remains the same when you remove more than half of the stock dimension in any plane; with less surface area making contact with either the fence or the tabletop, the stock has a tendency to lean and distort the profile. This can be extremely dangerous. Therefore, what looks like a project to make a simple picture frame is actually a guide to cutting deep rabbets accurately and safely.

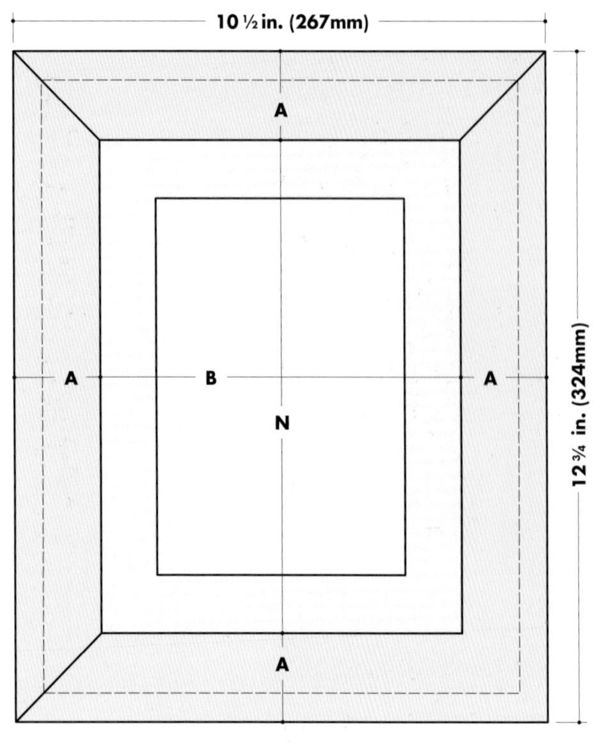


**Front Elevation**

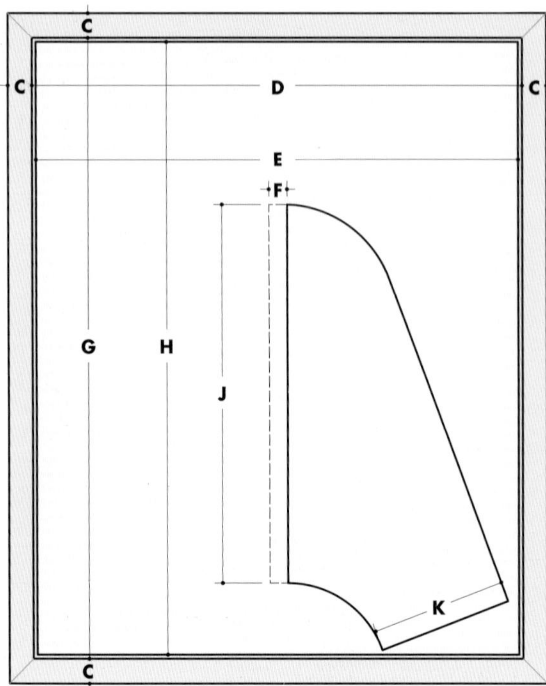


**Back Elevation**

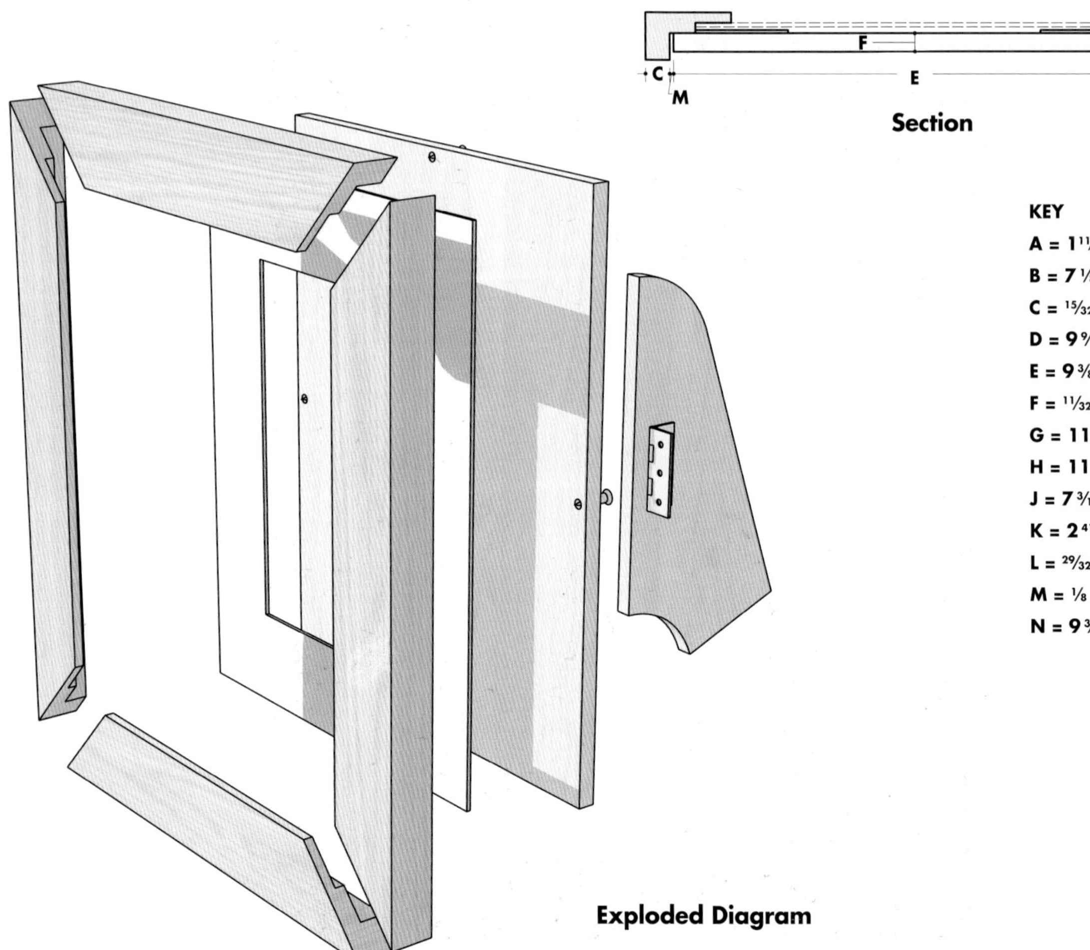


**Section**

**Exploded Diagram**

**KEY**

A = $1\tfrac{11}{16}$ in. (43mm)
B = $7\tfrac{1}{8}$ in. (181mm)
C = $\tfrac{15}{32}$ in. (12mm)
D = $9\tfrac{9}{16}$ in. (243mm)
E = $9\tfrac{3}{8}$ in. (239mm)
F = $\tfrac{11}{32}$ in. (9mm)
G = $11\tfrac{13}{16}$ in. (300mm)
H = $11\tfrac{21}{32}$ in. (296mm)
J = $7\tfrac{3}{16}$ in. (183mm)
K = $2\tfrac{41}{64}$ in. (67mm)
L = $\tfrac{29}{32}$ in. (23mm)
M = $\tfrac{1}{8}$ in. (2mm)
N = $9\tfrac{3}{8}$ in. (238mm)

1 Plane a length of stock for a supporting block, representing the amount of material removed from the first rabbet. Make an allowance for some double-sided tape along the face that will be parallel with the fence.

PICTURE FRAME

2 Apply the tape to the supporting block and press down firmly with a roller, avoiding any creases or contamination from wood chips.

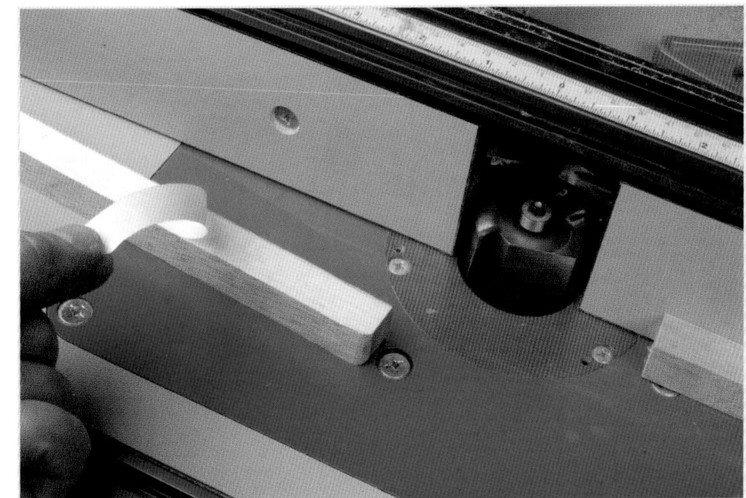

3 Attach the block to the fence and not the tabletop. If you need to make adjustments, the block will move with the fence. Round over the leading edge of the block on the outfeed side. You are now ready to cut the second rabbet, safe in the knowledge that the stock will remain supported throughout the operation.

4 To achieve perfect sets of miters with a minimum of equipment, cut the sides in pairs slightly oversize and trim one of each pair to the finished dimension on a shooting board with the 45° insert.

5 Use the two dimensioned pieces as templates to mark the next two. To avoid any confusion, mark each miter as you go when you are satisfied with the fit.

6 If you find that the miters still won't meet perfectly, try putting a strip of paper behind the back fence on the shooting board at the appropriate end to make a slight adjustment to the angle.

7 I find a strap clamp to be the most efficient means of clamping frames. It applies equal amounts of pressure to all four corners simultaneously.

8 Fit a back in the frame and attach a T-support.

*Your finished picture frame will look something like this.*

# MEAT TENDERIZER

I hope you will notice the similarity between this useful kitchen implement and those found in every workshop and find that the techniques transfer quite nicely to making something else. There are two main techniques in this project: the first will demonstrate how to create a round peg from a square section; the second will hone your sawing skills.

There's also a clever device called a foxed wedged tenon to attach the handle to the head.

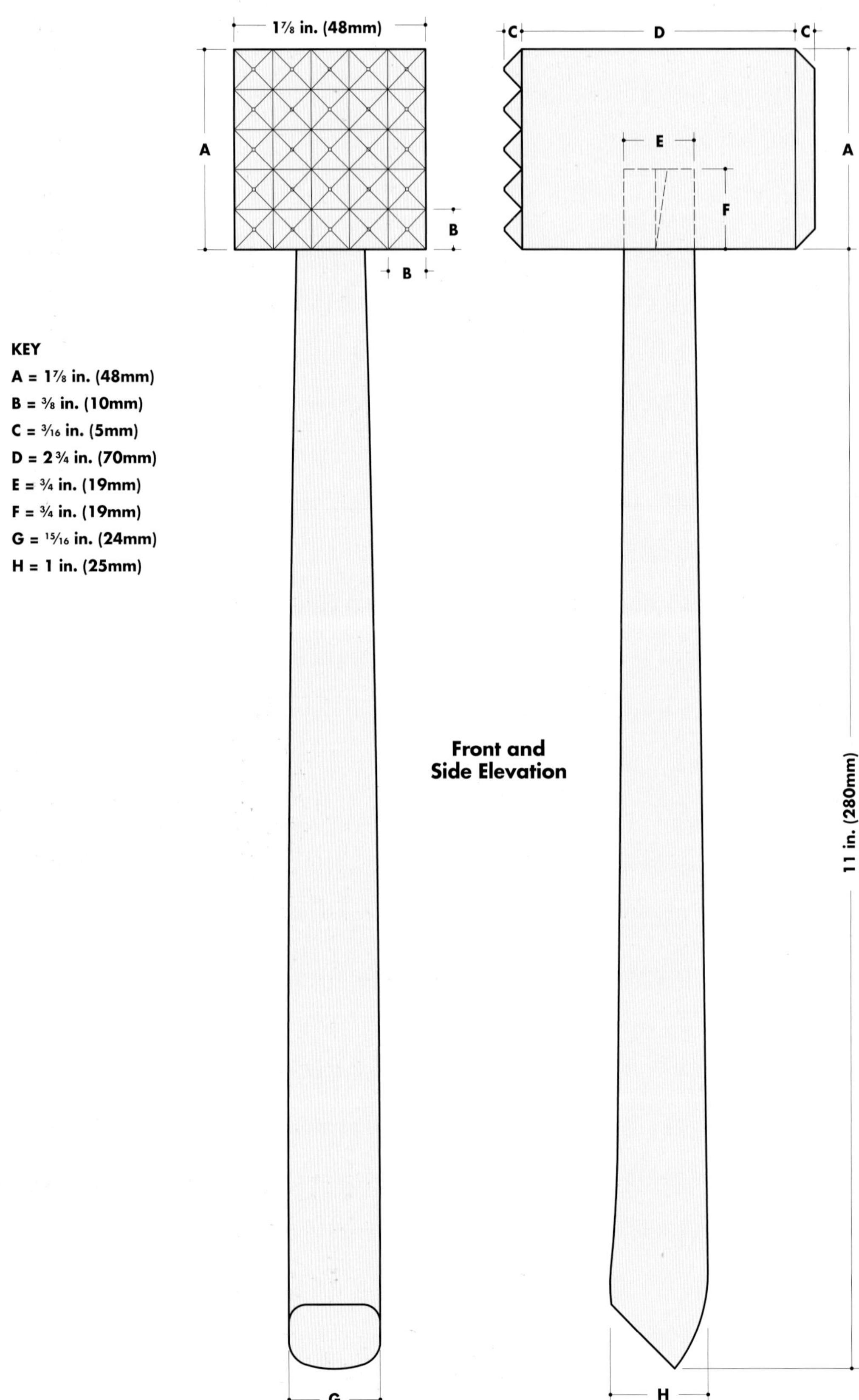


**Front and Side Elevation**

1 Hardwoods like beech, maple, and sycamore are ideal for making kitchen tools. Start off by drawing the shape of the handle and the diameter of the round tenon at one end to fit into the mortise.

2 While the stock is still square, cut a small V-shaped groove to take a wedge in the end of the handle to a depth equal to that of the hole on the head.

3 With a block plane, start to shape the handle by first removing the four corners and working your way around. It is important not to go beyond the circle marked on the end.

4 As soon as you are able to fit the end into the hole, draw around the handle to record how much of it can be inserted.

5 Using a rasp, continue to shape the handle without going above the line. Keep checking the fit until the handle reaches all the way to the bottom of the hole.

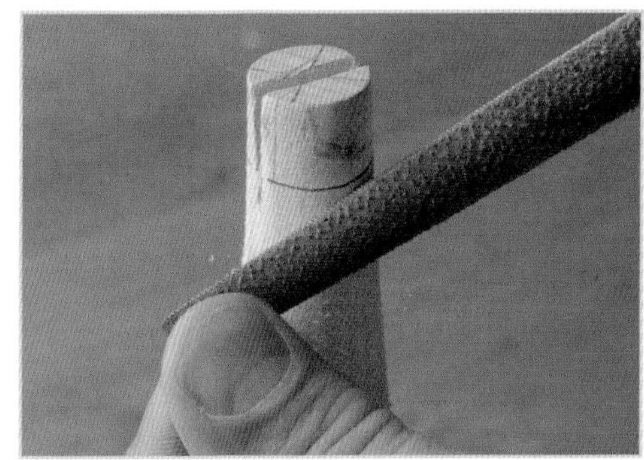

6 A set of convex scrapers can be used to feather the shape into the rest of the handle and remove all the marks from the rasp and plane.

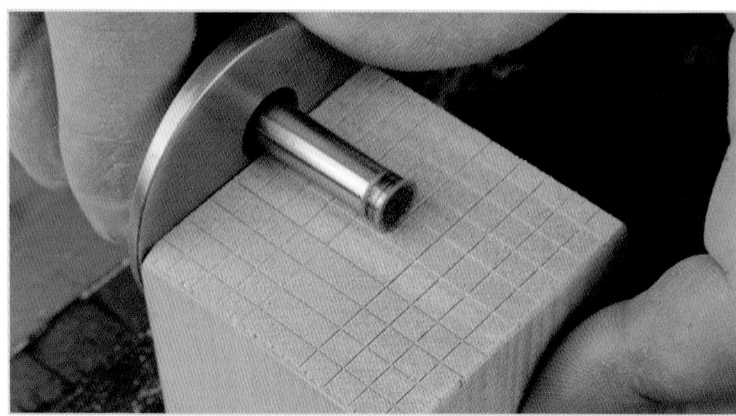

7 Using a marking gauge, section out the face of the hammer with equal spacing in both directions.

8 Using the finest saw you have – I used a Japanese saw – make cuts at 45° down to a base line equal to those on the hammer face.

9 Repeat the process in the other direction and from the other side to create a series of little pyramids.

10 Use the rasp to clean out the bottom of the trenches and adjust the tips of the pyramids to make them sharp.

11 The handle is held in place with a wedge made by paring a slice of wood against a block clamped to the bench.

**12** The wedge needs to be a reasonably tight fit so that it won't fit the V. It needs to be cut over-length by the same amount that it falls short of the bottom of the V.

All that remains now is to slot the handle with the wedge in position into the hammer head and knock it into place. The wedge will drive itself home and expand the tip of the handle. Get this right and there will be no need for glue.

*Your finished meat tenderizer will look something like this.*

# WEDGE-END BOX

This quadrant-shaped block of brown oak was left over from an earlier project. It had a few faults that made it unsuitable as a turning blank, and its size meant it was not viable for sawing into veneer, either. But it is not just the character of the material that can be a source of inspiration; the shape of an offcut can just as easily spark an idea.

When it comes to converting offcuts into a project made up of small components, it is a good idea to factor in the machining processes required and establish whether they can be carried out more efficiently while the original stock is still in one piece.

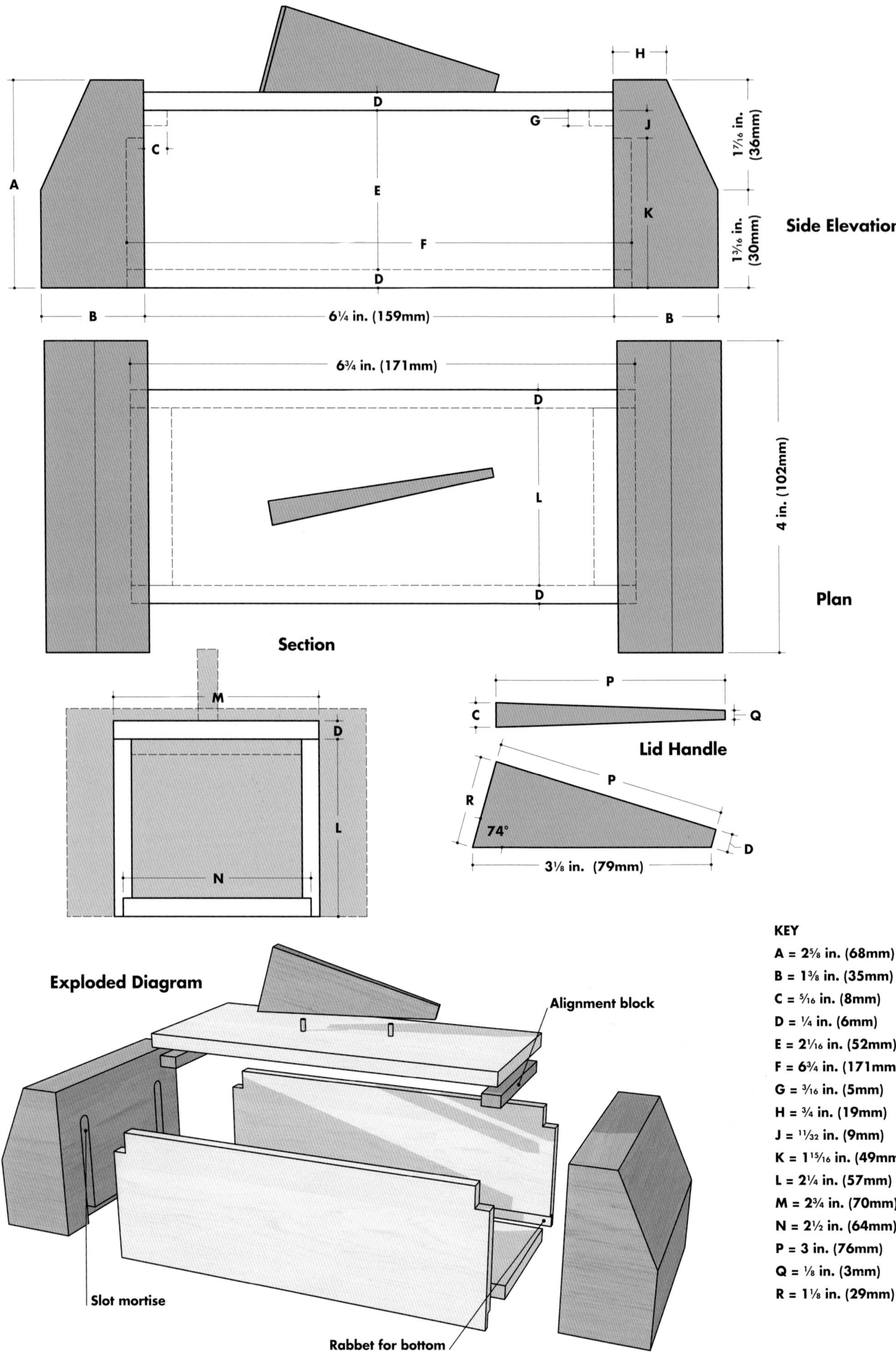
Side Elevation
A
B
C
D
E
F
G
H
J
K
1 7/16 in. (36mm)
1 3/16 in. (30mm)
6 1/4 in. (159mm)
Plan
6 3/4 in. (171mm)
L
4 in. (102mm)
Section
M
N
Lid Handle
P
Q
R
74°
3 1/8 in. (79mm)
Exploded Diagram
Alignment block
Slot mortise
Rabbet for bottom
KEY
A = 2 5/8 in. (68mm)
B = 1 3/8 in. (35mm)
C = 5/16 in. (8mm)
D = 1/4 in. (6mm)
E = 2 1/16 in. (52mm)
F = 6 3/4 in. (171mm)
G = 3/16 in. (5mm)
H = 3/4 in. (19mm)
J = 11/32 in. (9mm)
K = 1 15/16 in. (49mm)
L = 2 1/4 in. (57mm)
M = 2 3/4 in. (70mm)
N = 2 1/2 in. (64mm)
P = 3 in. (76mm)
Q = 1/8 in. (3mm)
R = 1 1/8 in. (29mm)

WEDGE-END BOX

1 The first step was to prepare a flat face and edge to the block from which all the joints could be machined.

2 The new growth was sawn from the block as close to the dark material as possible before planing by hand to reveal the rich grain.

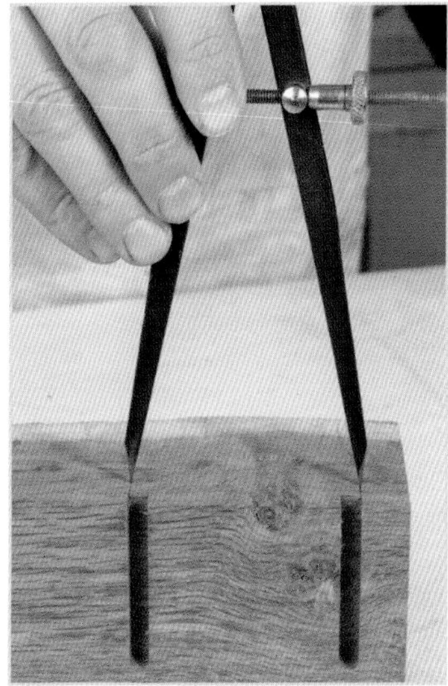

3 Having planed the material for the box sides to the same size as a router bit, I machined two grooves to take the sides on one end of the block. I recorded the spacing with a pair of dividers and transferred it to the other end of the block.

4 The grooves need to be cut shorter than the height of the box sides.

5 Slide a side piece into the groove and mark the depth of the groove at the top end of the side pieces.

6 Create a small shoulder by removing material from the top corner of each side piece.

7 Trim and mark each component for how they will fit together when the block is cut in two.

8 On the bottom of the block, machine rabbets between the grooves to take the bottom. Then cut the block in two and trim the ends to match.

9 Clamp the ends to the sides and prepare the bottom. This can be trimmed for a tight fit on the shooting board.

10 Make the lid and trim it to fit lengthwise, but leave it over-width. Glue a block to the underside of the lid to register it in place against one side. Leave the blocks over-length by about 1⁄16 in. (1 to 2mm).

**11** When the glue has dried, trim the blocks so that the lid sits flush.

**12** Mark the width of the lid from the other side and trim to finish.

*Your finished wedge-end box will look something like this.*

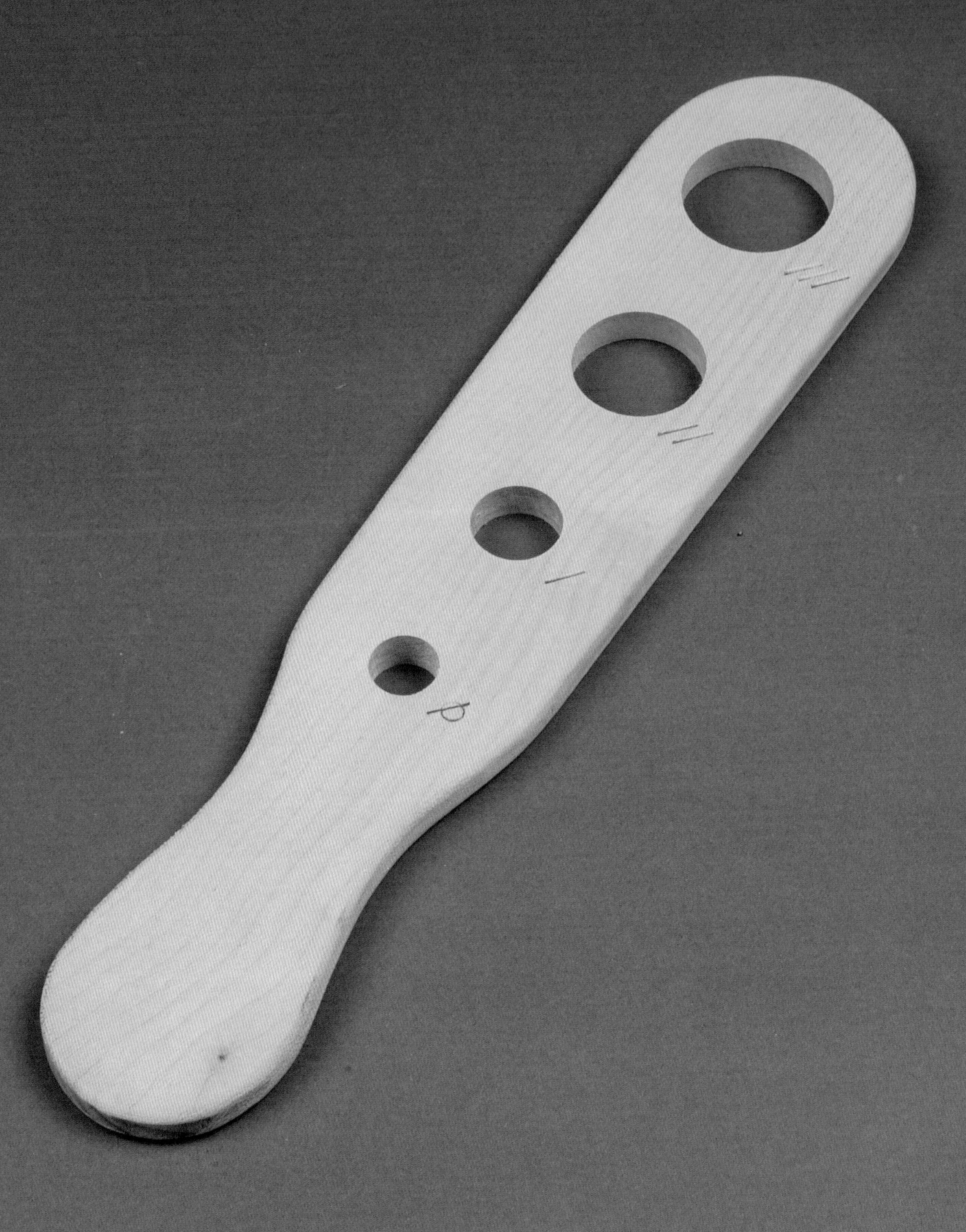

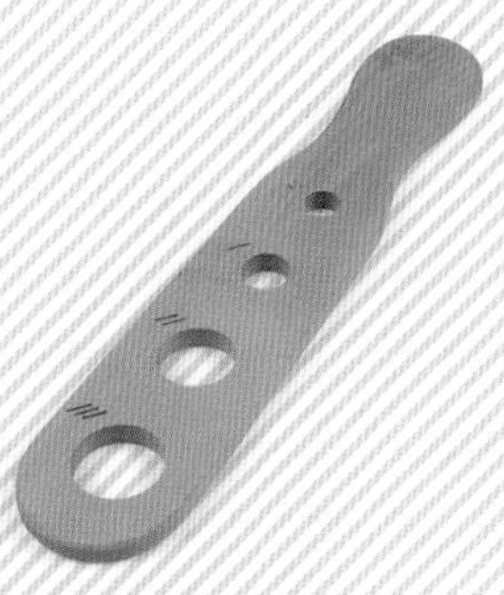

# SPAGHETTI GAUGE

This easy-to-use gauge provides a portion guide for one to four servings. There is nothing very complicated about the design of this popular kitchen utensil. However, looks can be deceiving: often the simplest objects require a disproportionate amount of skill and ingenuity to produce them efficiently. This project demonstrates how you can produce multiples of the same item from a single blank and incorporate some labor-saving techniques in the process.

Maple, beech, or sycamore would all be suitable species for this project. Make sure you have a razor-sharp bench plane at hand.

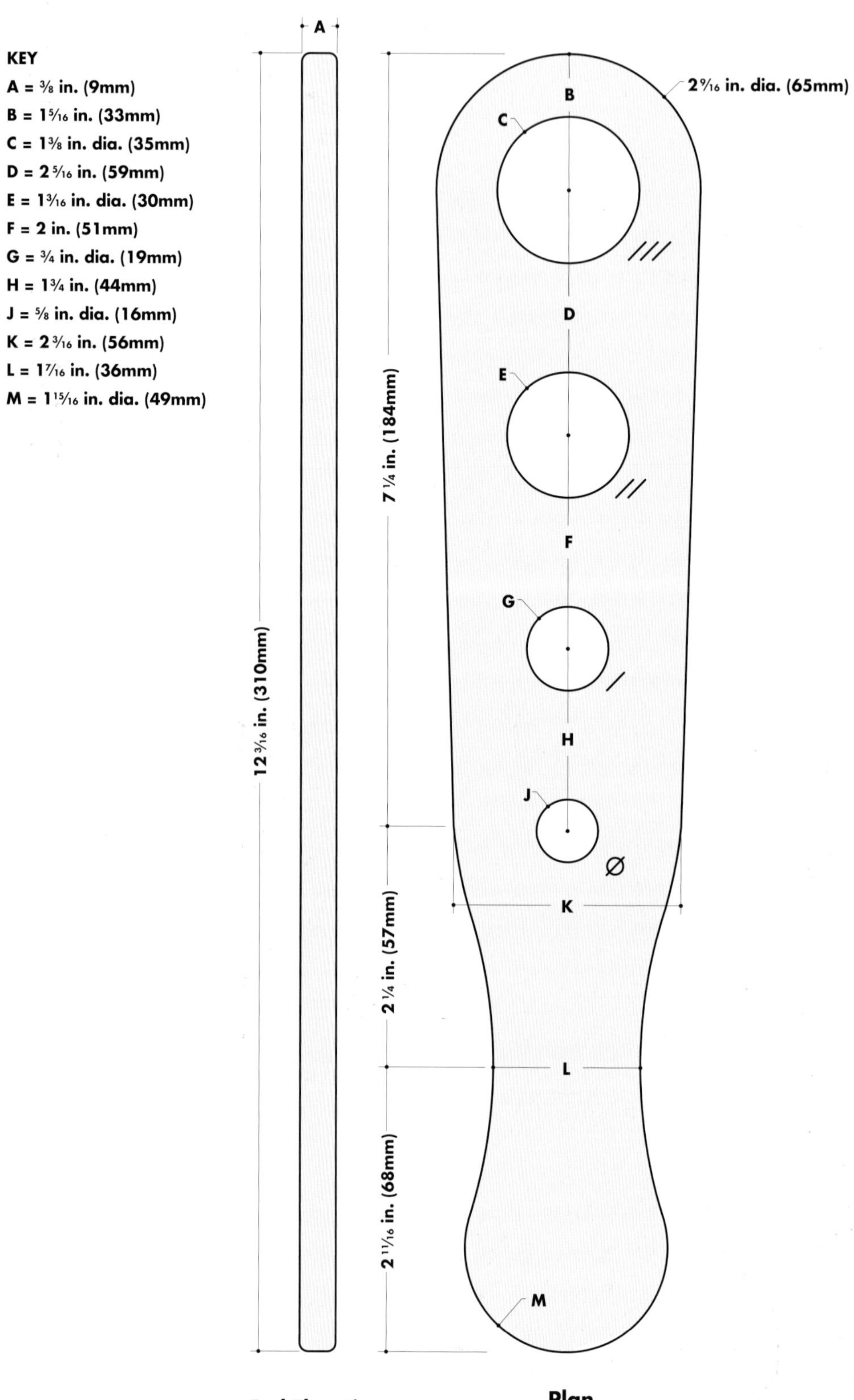
KEY
A = 3/8 in. (9mm)
B = 1 5/16 in. (33mm)
C = 1 3/8 in. dia. (35mm)
D = 2 5/16 in. (59mm)
E = 1 3/16 in. dia. (30mm)
F = 2 in. (51mm)
G = 3/4 in. dia. (19mm)
H = 1 3/4 in. (44mm)
J = 5/8 in. dia. (16mm)
K = 2 3/16 in. (56mm)
L = 1 7/16 in. (36mm)
M = 1 15/16 in. dia. (49mm)
A
12 3/16 in. (310mm)
7 1/4 in. (184mm)
2 1/4 in. (57mm)
2 11/16 in. (68mm)
2 9/16 in. dia. (65mm)
B
C
D
E
F
G
H
J
K
L
M
///
//
/
Ø
End Elevation
Plan

SPAGHETTI GAUGE

**1** Before marking out the shape of your gauge, plane your block so that it is square on all four long sides. Then mark out the set of holes using the information provided in the diagram opposite.

**2** There are a number of ways in which you can drill the holes: a drill press is best, but a hand drill will also cope quite well. Consider how many gauges you can get out of the block and drill the holes deep enough to accommodate a short batch run.

**3** Alternatively, drill the holes about $3/16$ in. (5mm) deeper than the thickness of the finished gauge. Take a slice off the block on the bandsaw or with a suitable handsaw, cutting through the holes as you go.

**4** Planing thin material is never easy; you will benefit from having a sharp plane to remove the saw marks on the cut surface. Work up against a bench stop that is thinner than the finished thickness of the gauge. Lift the plane off the gauge at the end of each stroke.

**5** Turn the gauge on its side in the vise and plane the edges flat to create the taper.

**6** The quickest way to shape the handle is to use an oscillating spindle sander after bandsawing off the corners. With a little practice, you will be able to create near-perfect arcs. The trick is to begin feeding the workpiece past the sanding drum in one direction and keep it moving. Ease onto the drum against the direction of rotation and ease off but don't stop in one place.

**7** A router mounted in a table is the quickest and safest method of working small components. Remove the square corners on the gauge using a ⅛-in. (3mm) round-over bit with a guide bearing. Just as with the oscillating spindle sander, make smooth, controlled passes in the opposite direction of the bit's rotation. Move the wood into the bit slowly in a glancing action and don't linger in one place.

**8** Use a chisel to make marks that indicate the portion sizes. Chop to a depth of about 1⁄16 in. (2mm) at 45 degrees to the direction of the grain to make the required number of V grooves.

*Your finished spaghetti gauge will look something like this.*

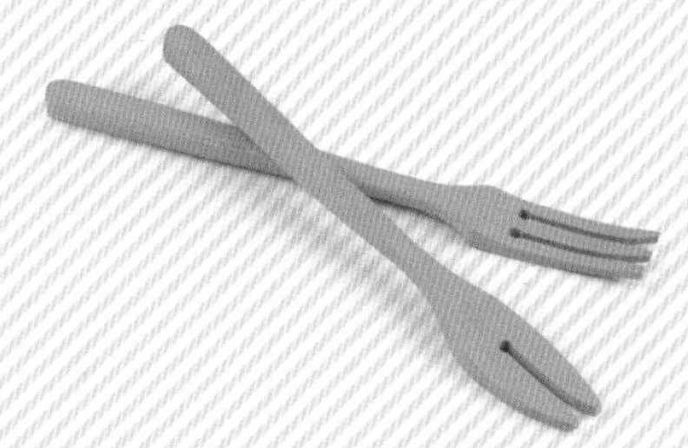

# SALAD SERVING FORKS

It is quite natural to take everyday objects for granted and not give a second thought as to how and why they are the way they are. Cutlery items, for example, have a number of functions that influence their design, so what better way to really get to know them than to make your own from scratch?

These implements may not be silver-service, but I guarantee you will never look at your knife and fork in the same way again once you have made these.

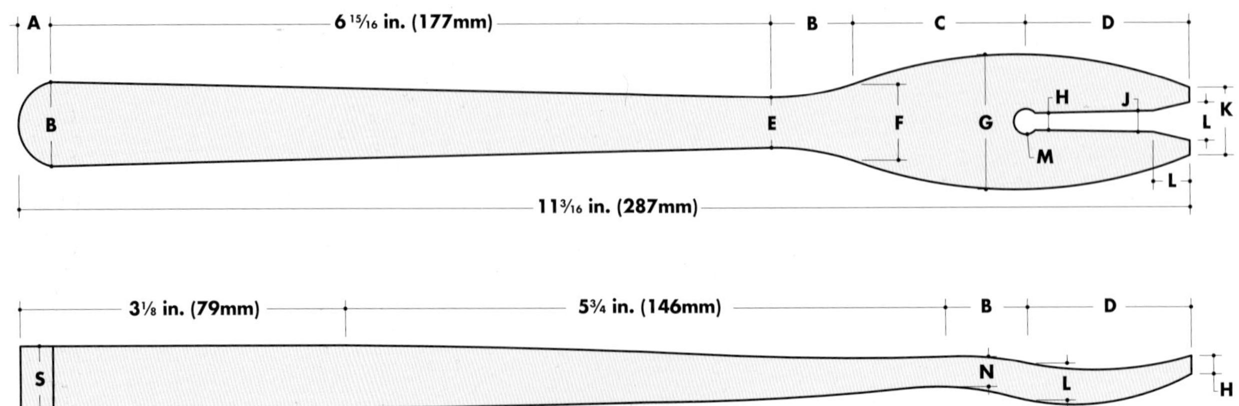


**Plan and Side Elevations**

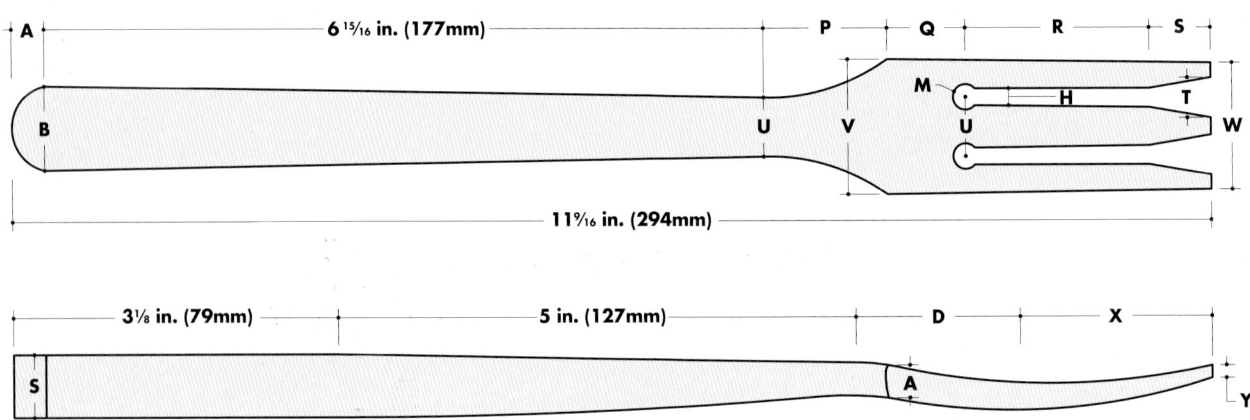


**KEY**

A = 5/16 in. (8mm)
B = 3/4 in. (19mm)
C = 1 11/16 in. (42mm)
D = 1 9/16 in. (40mm)
E = 15/32 in. (12mm)
F = 11/16 in. (18mm)
G = 1 1/4 in. (32mm)
H = 5/32 in. (4mm)

J = 3/16 in. (5mm)
K = 5/8 in. (16mm)
L = 11/32 in. (9mm)
M = 1/4 in. dia. (6mm)
N = 9/32 in. (7mm)
P = 1 3/16 in. (30mm)
Q = 3/4 in. (19mm)
R = 1 3/4 in. (44mm)

S = 5/8 in. (16mm)
T = 3/8 in. (10mm)
U = 9/16 in. (14mm)
V = 1 1/4 in. (32mm)
W = 1 3/16 in. (30mm)
X = 1 7/8 in. (48mm)
Y = 1/8 in. (3mm)

SALAD SERVING FORKS

1 You don't need a block big enough to make these utensils in pairs, but it will cut down on some of the work. You might be able to make two pairs from a thick block.

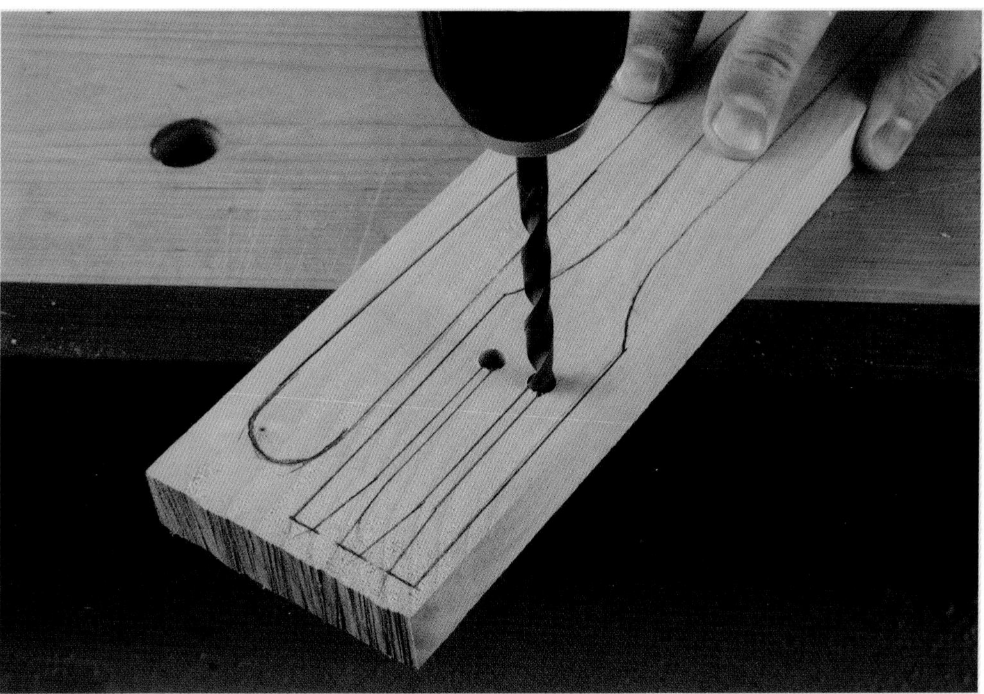

2 At the base of the tines, drill a hole slightly wider than the slot. This will keep you from having to finish these fiddly details with sandpaper and will help prevent splits.

3 Extend the lines that form the tines to the top edge of the block and saw down to the holes. Then rough-cut the components slightly oversize on the bandsaw.

5 A rasp is the perfect tool to shape the rest of the fork. Do as much of the shaping as you can while the piece still has some square edges, which makes it a little easier to clamp them in a vise.

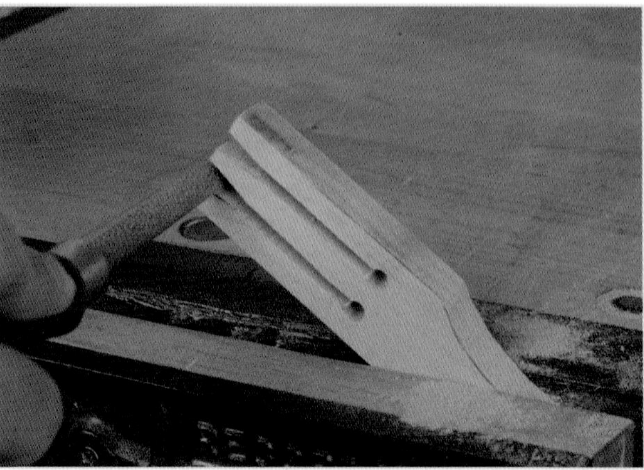

4 With a rasp, gently create the V-shape at the tip of the prongs. You could also use a chisel for this by laying the fork down flat on the bench.

6 Mark out the side profile of the forks and the scoop at the front to the desired taper. Don't be too severe with the shaping at the neck, because this will weaken the fork considerably.

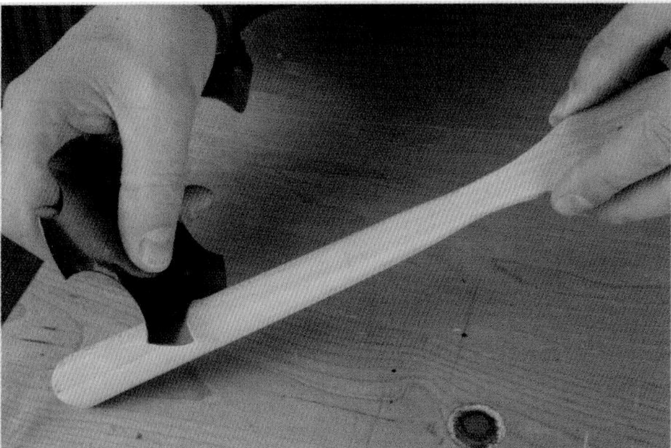

**7** If a simple round-over is used for the handle, then a rasp is the quickest way to achieve this…

**8** …followed by a convex scraper to smooth the surface.

*Your finished salad serving forks will look something like this.*

# DESK ORGANIZER

This project demonstrates how a seemingly random pile of offcuts can be transformed into something useful with the aid of a simple drilling jig. The measurements are not critical, because they will depend on the range of hole saws at your disposal. You will need at least two with a difference in size of around 5⁄16 in. (8mm). A drill press is the other essential piece of equipment for this project. Of course, if you own a lathe, you can turn these organizers from a stack of glued-up offcuts.

Making this project will transform unwanted scraps into a piece that is both beautiful and functional. If you have enough offcuts you could, of course, make a set as we have done here.

## Elevations and Plans

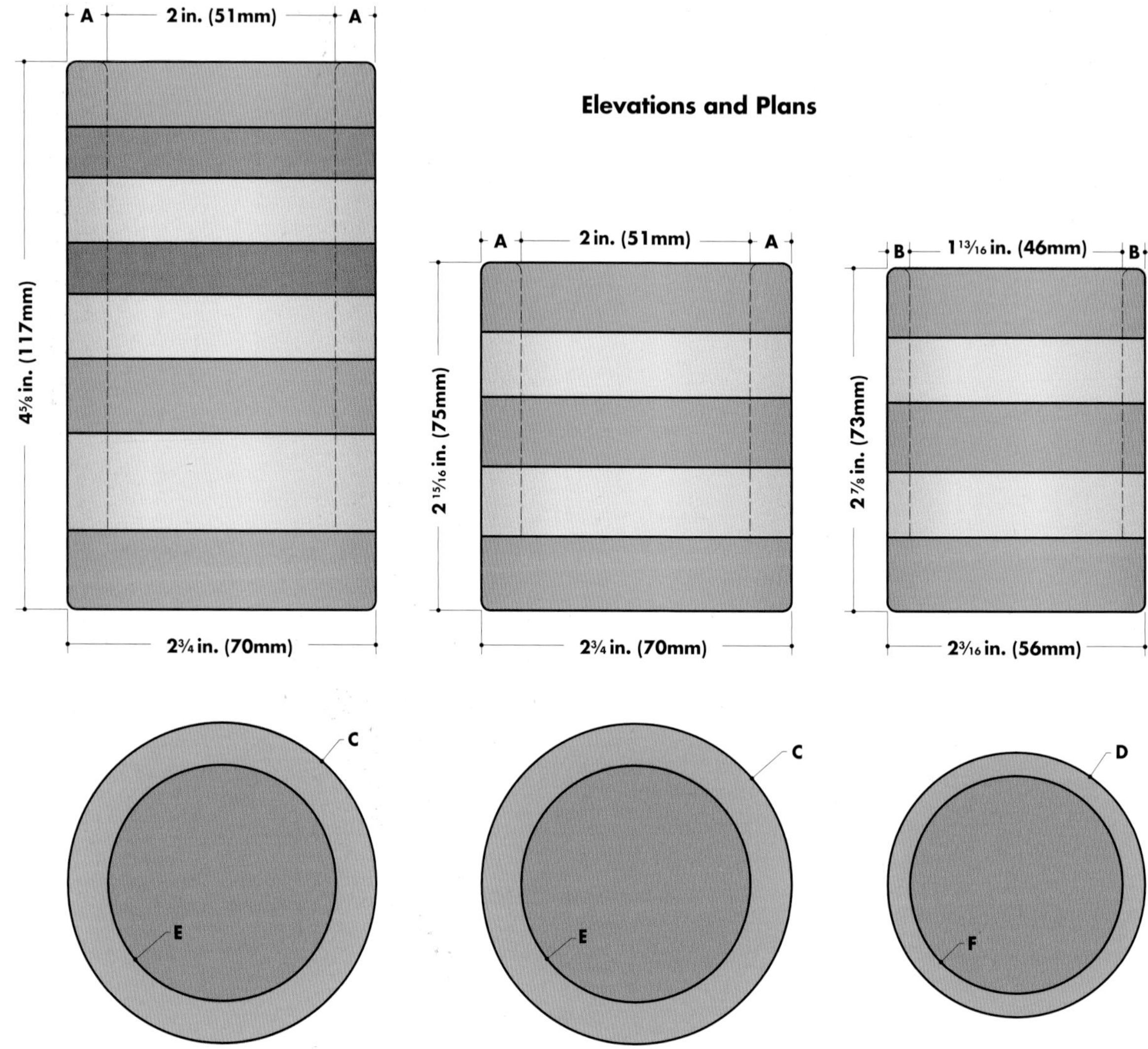


**KEY**

A = ⅜ in. (10mm)

B = 3⁄16 in. (5mm)

C = 2¾ in. dia. (70mm)

D = 2 3⁄16 in. dia. (56mm)

E = 2 in. dia. (51mm)

F = 1 13⁄16 in. dia. (46mm)

**1** Make sure that you use offcuts that have parallel faces and two edges cut square at an angle of 90°.

**2** Attach two battens at 90° on to a board that is large enough to extend beyond the perimeter of the table on your drill press.

**3** Clamp the jig to the table. Using the two square edges for reference, place an offcut in the jig and cut a hole using the smaller of the two hole saws.

**4** When you have completed the set, go back and drill again with the larger hole saw.

**5** The result will be a ring. Unless you have the option to fit a long centering drill in the chuck, go very slowly at first because the hole-saw will not have a guide.

6 On an upturned belt sander, remove any splinters but keep the two flat surfaces parallel.

7 Glue the rings together to form a tube of the desired height for whatever you'd like to store in it.

8 When the stack is dry, return to the belt sander and round off the outside.

9 Use a rasp to remove the worst of the bumps on the inside.

10 An oscillating spindle sander is the quickest way to smooth the interior.

**11** Use the bandsaw to cut a slightly oversize bottom for the tube and glue it in place.

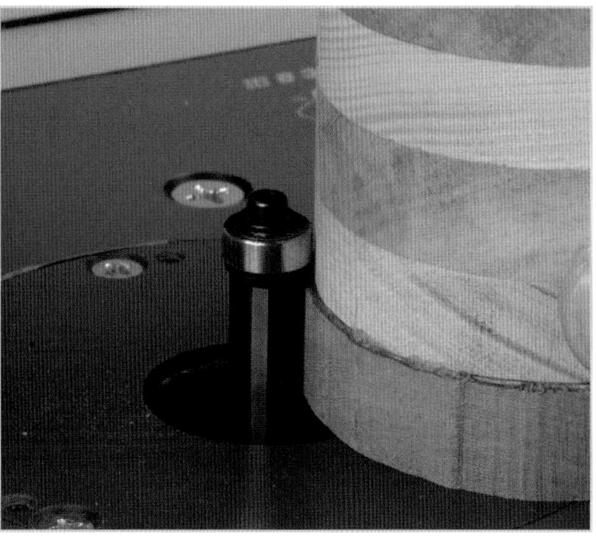

**12** Use a bearing-guided bit in a router to trim the bottom flush with the tube.

*Your finished set of desk organizers will look something like this.*

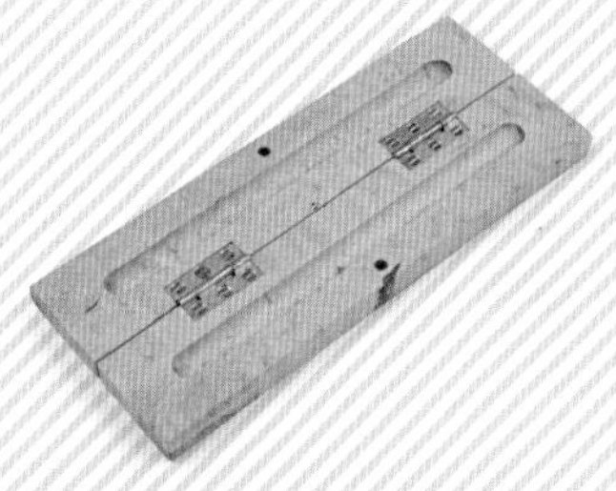

# PEN CASE

A fundamental aspect of cabinetmaking is the fitting of hardware such as hinges and locks into a frame or carcase. In principle, the technique is to mark around the component and remove enough waste so that it can sit in the recess.

In practice, there is a little more to think about before you can tackle the job without fear of ruining a perfectly good piece of work. This project is less about cabinet work – although perfectly square stock is essential – and more about accurate marking and drilling. You will also need a pair of rare-earth magnets and two hinges to complete this project.

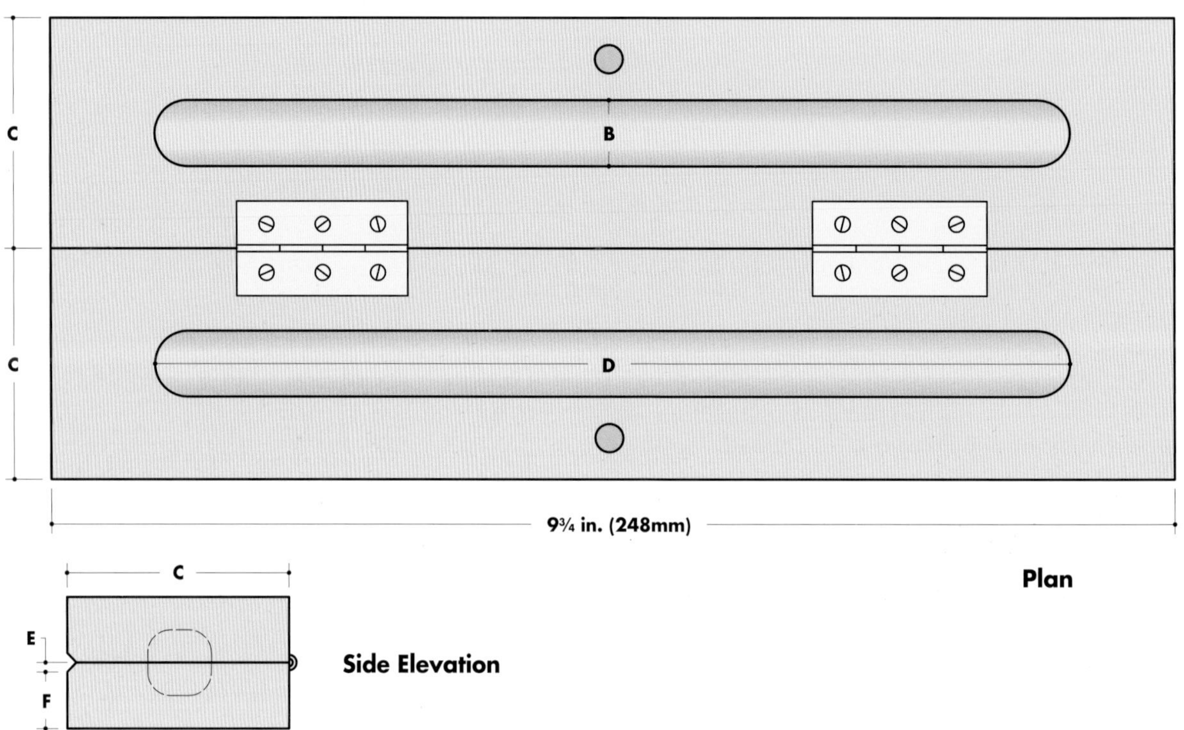


C
E
F

Side Elevation

Plan

**KEY**

**A = $1\frac{1}{8}$ in. (29mm)**
**B = $\frac{1}{2}$ in. (13mm)**
**C = $1\frac{15}{16}$ in. (49mm)**
**D = $7\frac{7}{8}$ in. (200mm)**
**E = $\frac{1}{16}$ in. (2mm)**
**F = $\frac{1}{2}$ in. (13mm)**

**1** Use a dish-carving bit for the groove. Unlike a core box bit, which has a round bottom, this one has a flat bottom that allows you to widen the cut without leaving ripples. The edges of the groove will still have curved corners.

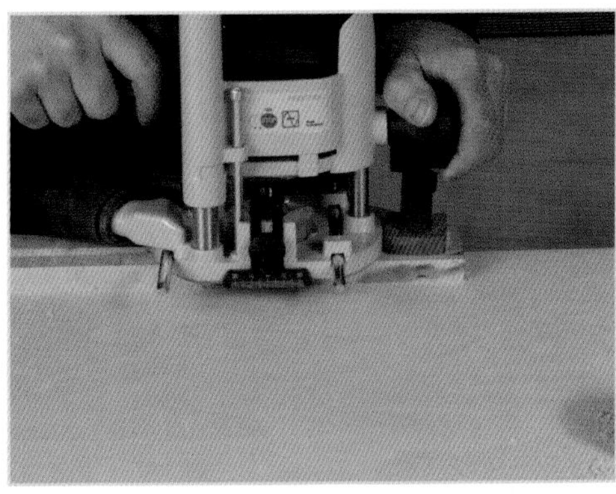

**2** Using the guide fence, set the router to cut grooves using the edge of the base plate as a reference and a clamp to act as a stop. It might be easier to machine two grooves while the stock is still in one piece.

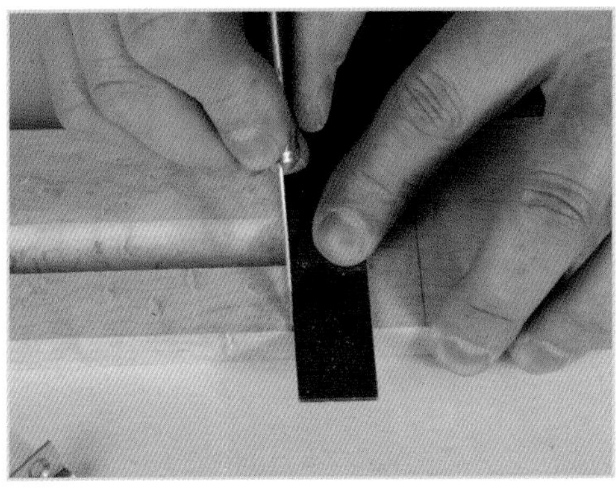

**3** Select a position for your hinges and make a single knife mark. Place the hinge directly on top of the mark and mark a second line at the other end. There is no need to mark the full depth of the hinge – only the width.

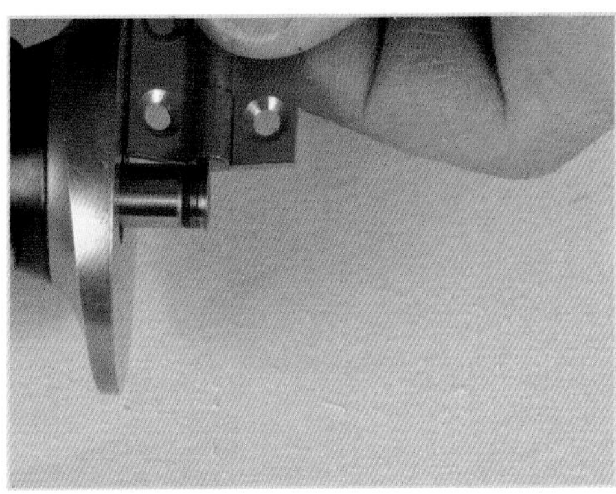

**4** Set a marking gauge from the edge of one leaf to slightly less than the center of the knuckle.

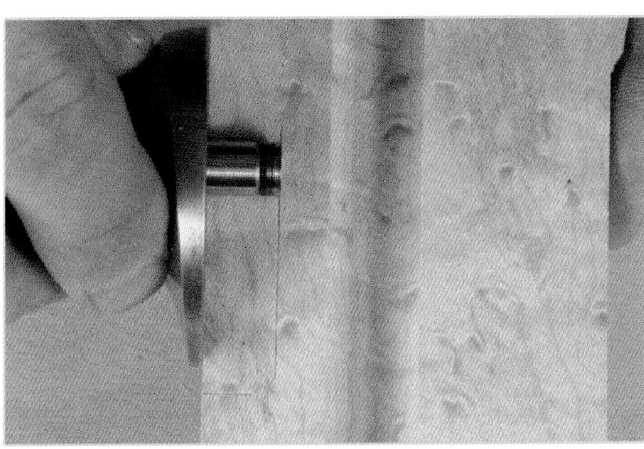

**5** Transfer this line to the stock. Note that it is not important for the lines to meet.

6 Using a router set to the depth of the hinge flap, remove most of the waste freehand, leaving a small amount to remove with a chisel.

7 Clear out the rest of the waste with a chisel, working up to the line a little at a time.

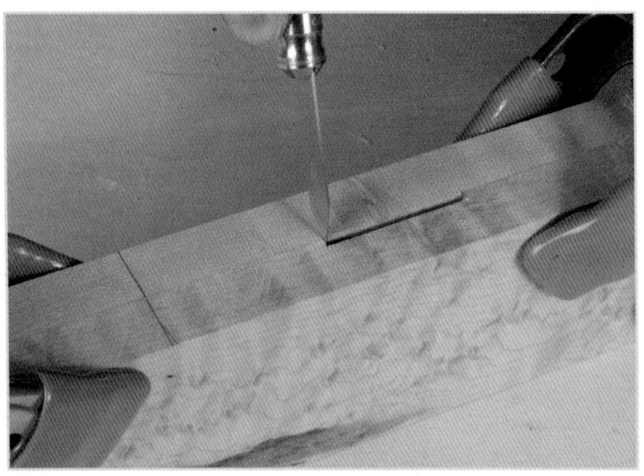

8 When you have completed one side, clamp the two halves together and then mark out for the corresponding hinge flaps.

9 Use spring clamps to pinch the two halves together and check the fit of the hinges before drilling any screw holes.

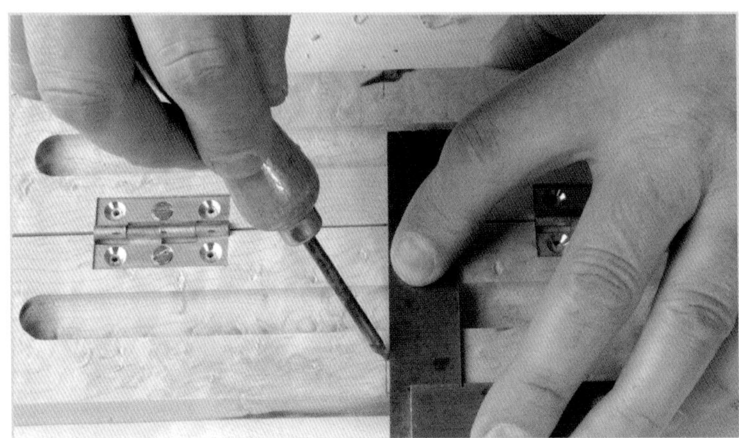

10 Mark a centerline to drill the small blind holes for the rare-earth magnets.

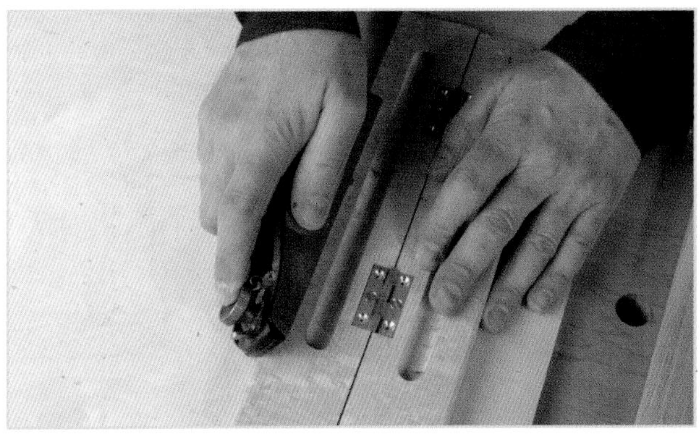

**11** Apply a small chamfer to the front inside edges and cut the box to length while it is assembled.

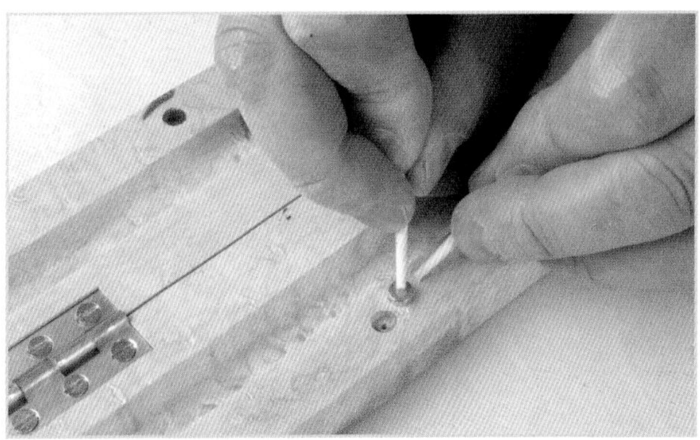

**12** Unless the magnets are a tight fit, they will require a little epoxy to hold them in place. Use a couple of wooden pegs to maneuver them into their holes.

*Your finished pen case will look something like this.*

# FLOATING SHELF

Shelves are sometimes required to fulfill more than one function; they have to support the objects placed on them while being a feature in their own right. The hardware used to hold shelves in place can be unattractive, so the answer is to conceal it within the shelf and create what might be called a floating shelf.

This project introduces the principles of basic box construction. There are no complex joints or special dowels used – just plain, old-fashioned double rabbets to maximize the gluing area of the straight-grain wood and minimize the weaker endgrain. This joint can be used to reinforce large pieces of furniture where strength is required.

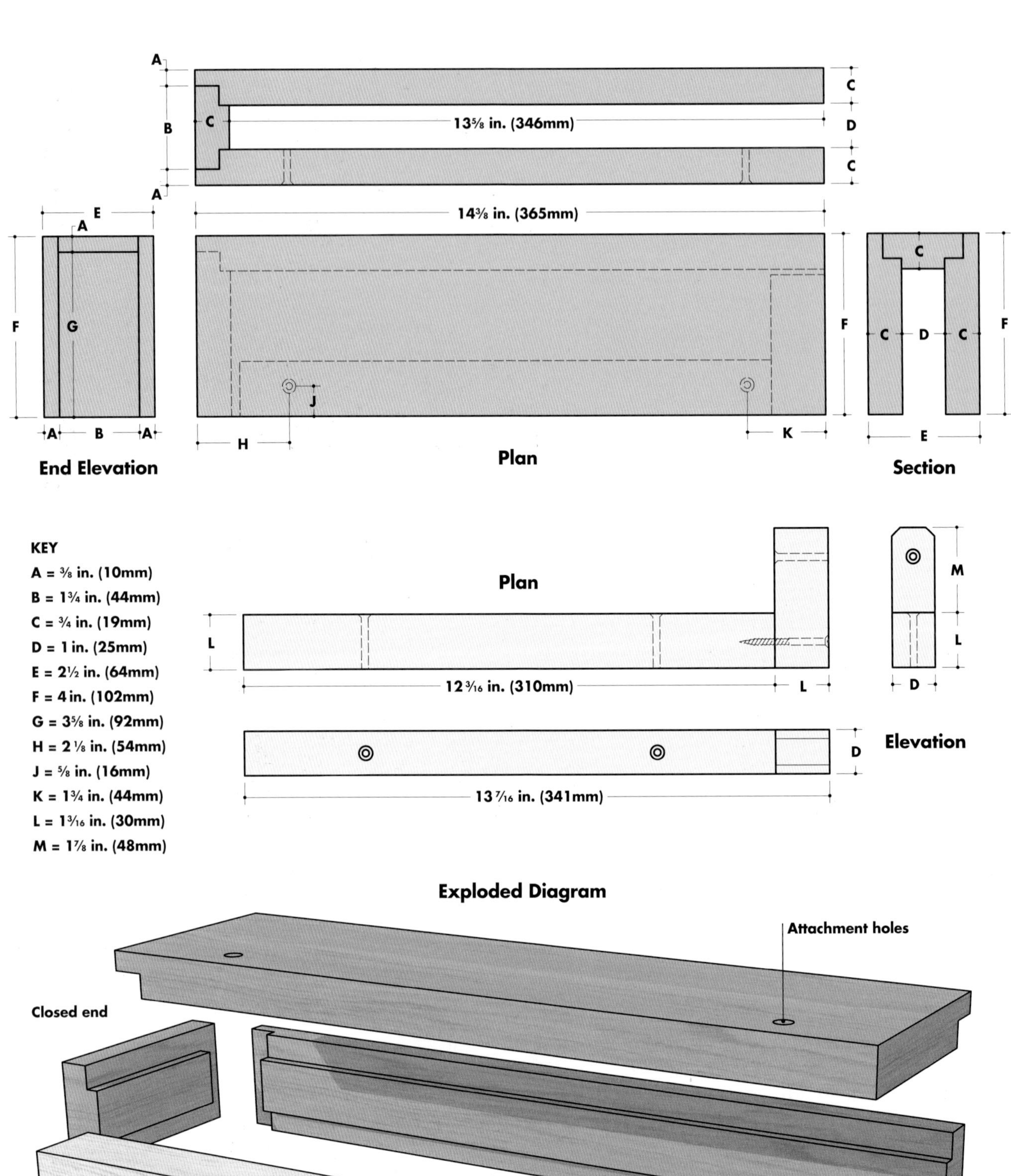

A
B
C
A
13 5/8 in. (346mm)
C
D
C
E
A
F
G
A
B
A
End Elevation
14 3/8 in. (365mm)
F
J
H
K
Plan
C
F
C
D
C
F
E
Section
KEY
A = 3/8 in. (10mm)
B = 1 3/4 in. (44mm)
C = 3/4 in. (19mm)
D = 1 in. (25mm)
E = 2 1/2 in. (64mm)
F = 4 in. (102mm)
G = 3 5/8 in. (92mm)
H = 2 1/8 in. (54mm)
J = 5/8 in. (16mm)
K = 1 3/4 in. (44mm)
L = 1 3/16 in. (30mm)
M = 1 7/8 in. (48mm)
Plan
L
12 3/16 in. (310mm)
L
M
L
D
D
Elevation
13 7/16 in. (341mm)
Exploded Diagram
Attachment holes
Closed end
Open end
Wall-mounting batten
Return batten

**1** Start by machining a rabbet on the inside edge of the top and bottom pieces. You don't have to be too concerned with the dimensions – approximately half the thickness of the stock in one direction and visibly more in the other. I find this method makes it easy to identify the orientation of components.

FLOATING SHELF

**2** If you are working to a specific thickness of shelf, you can now prepare the front section. Hold it in the rabbets and mark the second part of the rabbet.

**3** Note that the amount of material above the top edge as it appears in this photo is the fence setting for your router table.

**4** The bit height remains the same as long as you machine the workpiece on its edge.

**5** For best results when machining joints, always use hold-downs or feather boards to maintain a constant profile. This is also the safest method.

6 This router setting will be the same for the ends of the top and bottom of your shelf. Use a cross-cut miter gauge to support the work.

7 You should be able to trim the ends of the front piece by hand with a saw.

8 You should now have a complete set of components to make a shelf with a closed end.

9 For a shelf with one end butting up to a wall, just trim the end flush.

10 After gluing up the shelf, make a suitable batten to attach it to the wall. Chamfer the edge of the return batten to make it easier to slide on the shelf.

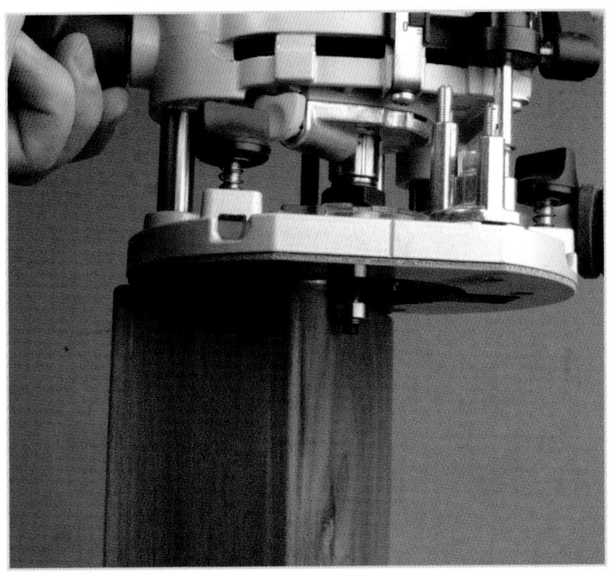

**11** To soften the edge of the shelf, you can run around the corners with a trim router fitted with a small roundover cutter or 45° chamfer bit.

**12** Finally, drill and countersink for small screws in the top of the shelf to attach it to the batten.

*Your finished floating shelf will look something like this.*

# COLLECTOR'S TRAY

What are often referred to as collector's trays are typically drawer dividers that were once used to contain the individual pieces of metal type used for printing. For those of us with organized minds, the thought of rows of neat compartments in which to store and display our precious possessions is very appealing.

This project centers around the biscuit jointer, although a plunge saw or miter saw with trenching ability could be used just as effectively.

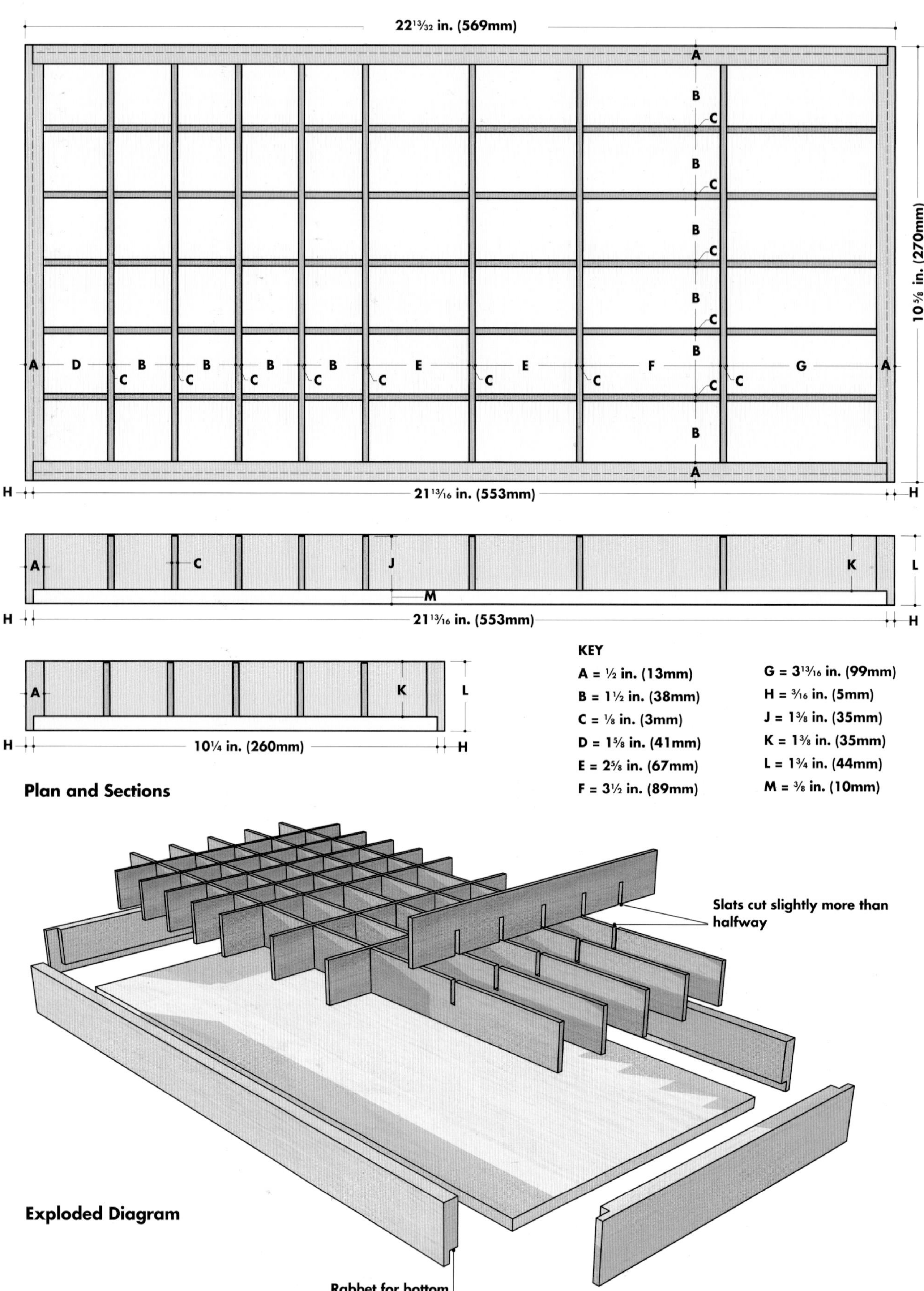
22 13/32 in. (569mm)
10 5/8 in. (270mm)
21 13/16 in. (553mm)
A
B
C
D
E
F
G
H
J
K
L
M
10 1/4 in. (260mm)
KEY
A = 1/2 in. (13mm)
B = 1 1/2 in. (38mm)
C = 1/8 in. (3mm)
D = 1 5/8 in. (41mm)
E = 2 5/8 in. (67mm)
F = 3 1/2 in. (89mm)
G = 3 13/16 in. (99mm)
H = 3/16 in. (5mm)
J = 1 3/8 in. (35mm)
K = 1 3/8 in. (35mm)
L = 1 3/4 in. (44mm)
M = 3/8 in. (10mm)
Plan and Sections
Slats cut slightly more than halfway
Exploded Diagram
Rabbet for bottom

1 Determine the width of the cut from your blade by creating a groove in a piece of scrap with a single pass. Then use the groove as a gauge to prepare sufficient material for the dividers. They should fit in the groove cleanly and without resistance.

2 From squared stock with one side milled to the same height as the material used for the dividers, make up a bracket with the two components joined at 90°.

3 Set the depth of cut on your machine to just over half the width of the material used for the dividers. A miter saw needs to be set to cut a trench.

**4** Attach a fence to the top of your bracket, set back from the edge of one side, and use it to produce a cut with your machine. You will not need this jig if you are using a miter saw.

**5** Before you can establish the precise length of the strips used for the dividers, you need to create the walls for the tray. One method is to cut a rabbet with a router.

**6** It is not important to have the bottom board cut exactly to size just yet; in fact, it may make things more difficult if you have. Set your rabbet to about half the thickness of the material used for the walls.

**7** Cut the two sets of dividers slightly overlong and tape them together. Try to use the same amount of tape at each end of the bundle so that it remains square against any fence that you might use.

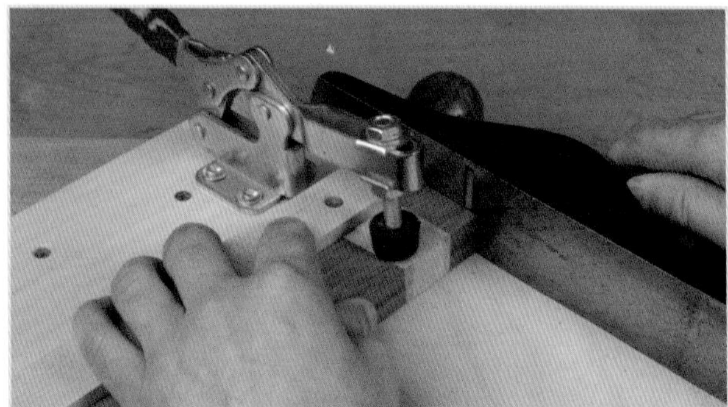

**8** Using the shooting board, trim the bundle at one end to obtain a clean square edge from which to generate center lines for each divider. Unless an overall dimension for the tray is critical, you can leave the bundles slightly overlong; $\frac{1}{32}$ to $\frac{1}{16}$ in. (1 to 2 mm) should be enough.

**9** Using the center lines for the dividers, position the bundles in the jig so that the line corresponds with the middle of the cut on the bracket.

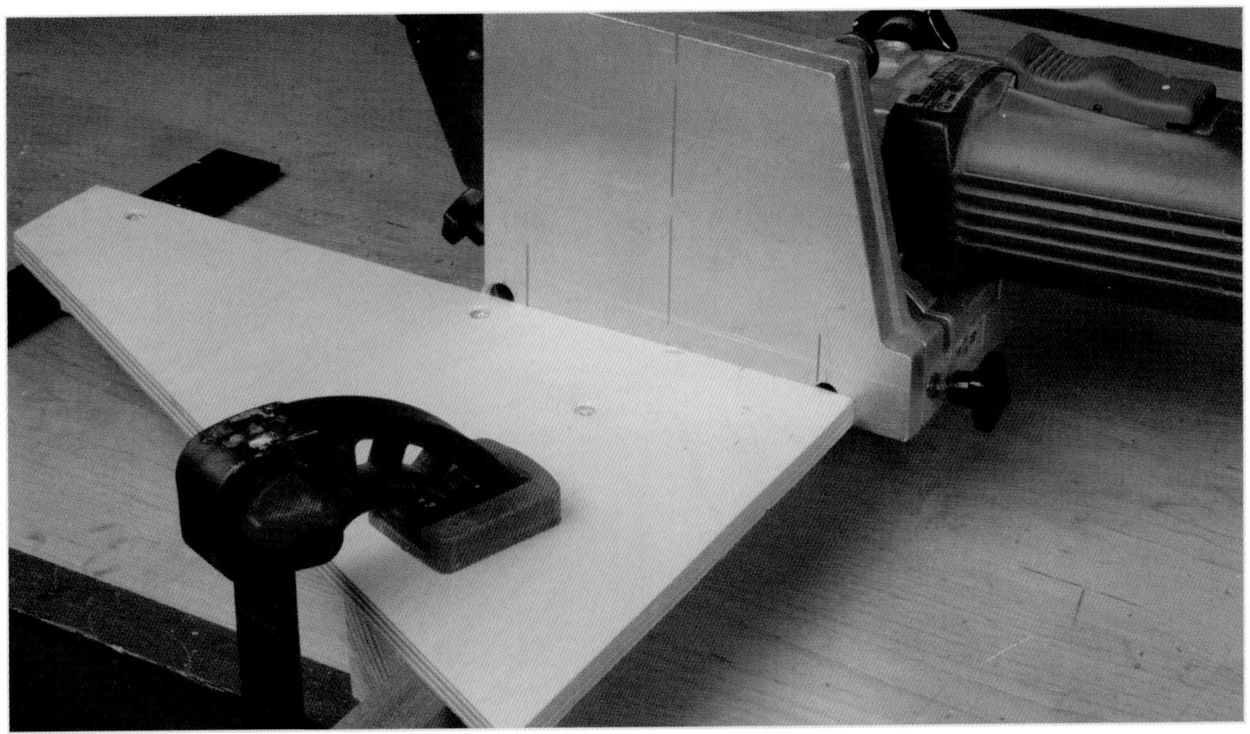

**10** Clamp the jig to the bench and complete the cuts on both bundles of dividers. Using a center line as your reference means you can work from each end of the bundle and not have to worry about which side of the line to make the cut.

**11** Remove the tape from both bundles and number them clearly at one end before assembling. Any under-cut will be difficult to correct, so you might want to plane the tops or bottoms of each divider for a flush fit.

**12** Build up the pattern of dividers and clamp two opposing walls of the frame to the ends. Measure between the rabbets to determine what the finished dimensions of the bottom board will be.

13 Clamp the two walls to the bottom board and adjust any discrepancy in the length of the components.

14 Now complete the joints by rabbeting the ends of the last two wall pieces.

15 Glue the walls to the bottom board, making sure they remain at 90°.

**16** Insert the dividers in the tray in the numbered sequence. If you need to make any adjustments in length, do it at the same end of each divider in turn, using a shooting board.

*Your finished collector's tray will look something like this.*

# SLIDING DOVETAIL BOX

This is a tried-and-tested design for a small box that more commonly features a tongue and groove to locate the lid into the box base. The principle for this version is much the same but requires some really fine adjustment on the router table and careful marking out beforehand. The lid and the box base are made from the same block of material, so it is possible to maintain the figuring of the grain between the two components and create an almost invisible joint. This project includes instructions on how to make three different sizes of box.

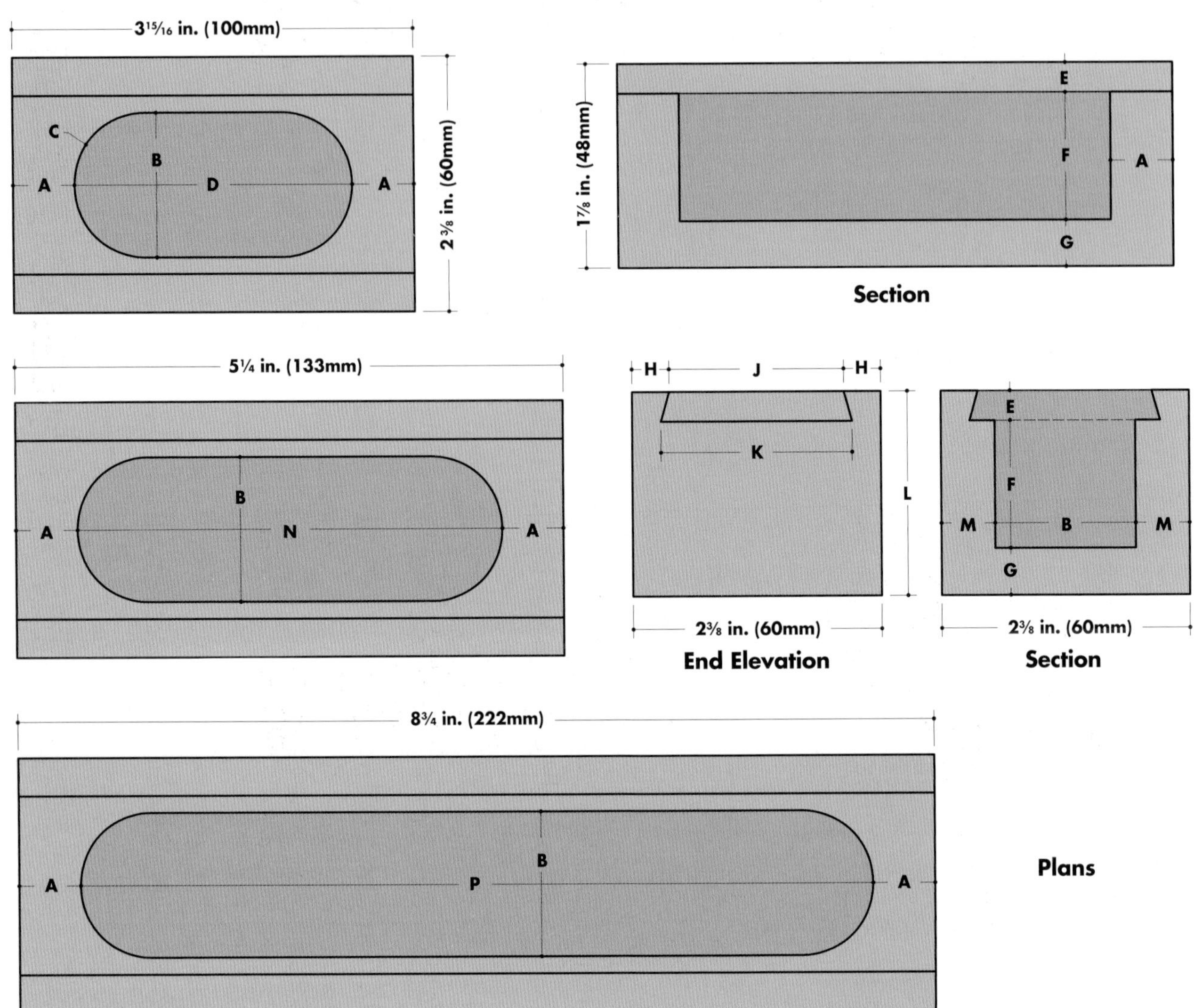


**KEY**

A = ⁵⁄₈ in. (16mm)
B = 1³⁄₈ in. (35mm)
C = 1³⁄₈ in. dia. (35mm)
D = 2 ¹¹⁄₁₆ in. (68mm)
E = ¹⁄₄ in. (6mm)
F = 1³⁄₁₆ in. (30mm)
G = ⁷⁄₁₆ in. (11mm)
H = ³⁄₈ in. (10mm)
J = 1⁵⁄₈ in. (41mm)
K = 1¹³⁄₁₆ in. (46mm)
L = 1⁷⁄₈ in. (48mm)
M = ¹⁄₂ in. (13mm)
N = 4 in. (102mm)
P = 7¹⁄₂ in. (191mm)

**1** Prepare a block with square sides and faces; mark it so that when you resaw it to separate the top from the base, the components can be realigned in the same orientation.

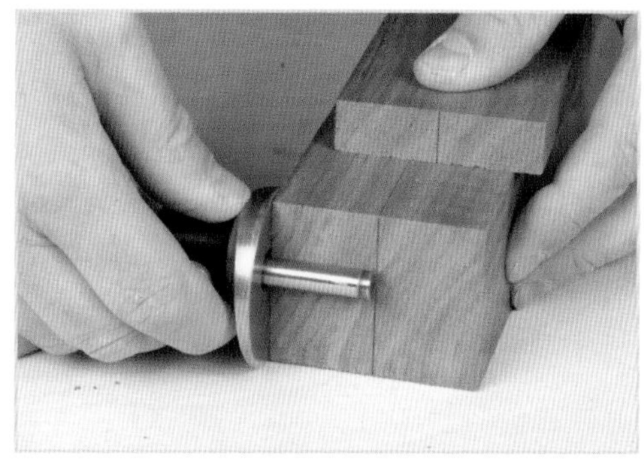

**2** Now mark a center line on the ends of both components and the top edge of the box base.

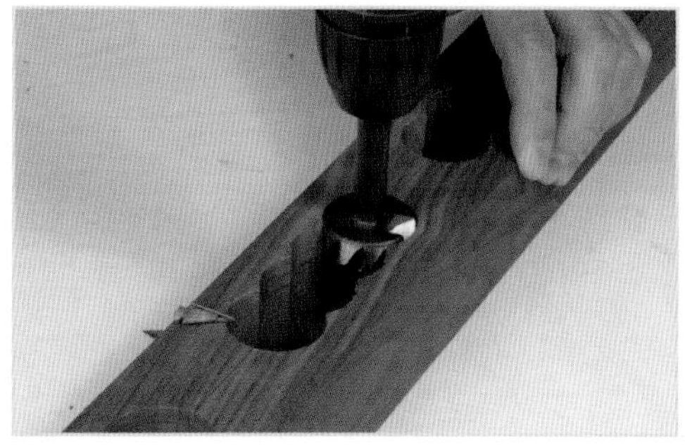

**3** With a large Forstner bit, drill repeat blind holes to hollow out the box. If you have sufficient material, make more than one box at a time. Drill accurately along the center line.

**4** Clean out the inside walls of the void with a chisel and finish off with a rasp. It is not necessary to square the corners unless you are making a container for a specific purpose.

**5** Using your router table, remove sufficient waste from the top of the box base to a depth that will accommodate the lid.

6 Level the surface with a shoulder plane. Do not use sandpaper. You will need clean sharp edges for the dovetail joint.

7 Go back to the router table and machine a dovetail profile on the inside edges of the wall along the length of the rabbet. Creep up on the depth of cut very slowly to avoid cutting into the bottom of the rabbet.

8 Clamp the lid to the top of the box base and align the center lines. Mark a line from the widest point of the dovetail wall onto the lid. This will determine the maximum width of the lid.

9 Cut the lid to the width required and create a dovetail profile on one edge. As before, creep up on the depth of cut to avoid reducing the width of the lid. To maintain the figure of the grain, mark the ends of the board to avoid machining the wrong way up.

10 The best fit at this stage is tight across the width with a small amount of clearance on the bottom edge.

**11** If the lid is tight in the joint, plane the top edge of the box base so that the lid can effectively drop down into the slot. These are very fine adjustments, so set the plane to remove the finest shaving possible. When you are satisfied with the fit, plane the lid until it is flush with the box base.

**12** With the lid in place, cut the individual boxes from the block.

*Your finished sliding dovetail boxes will look something like this.*

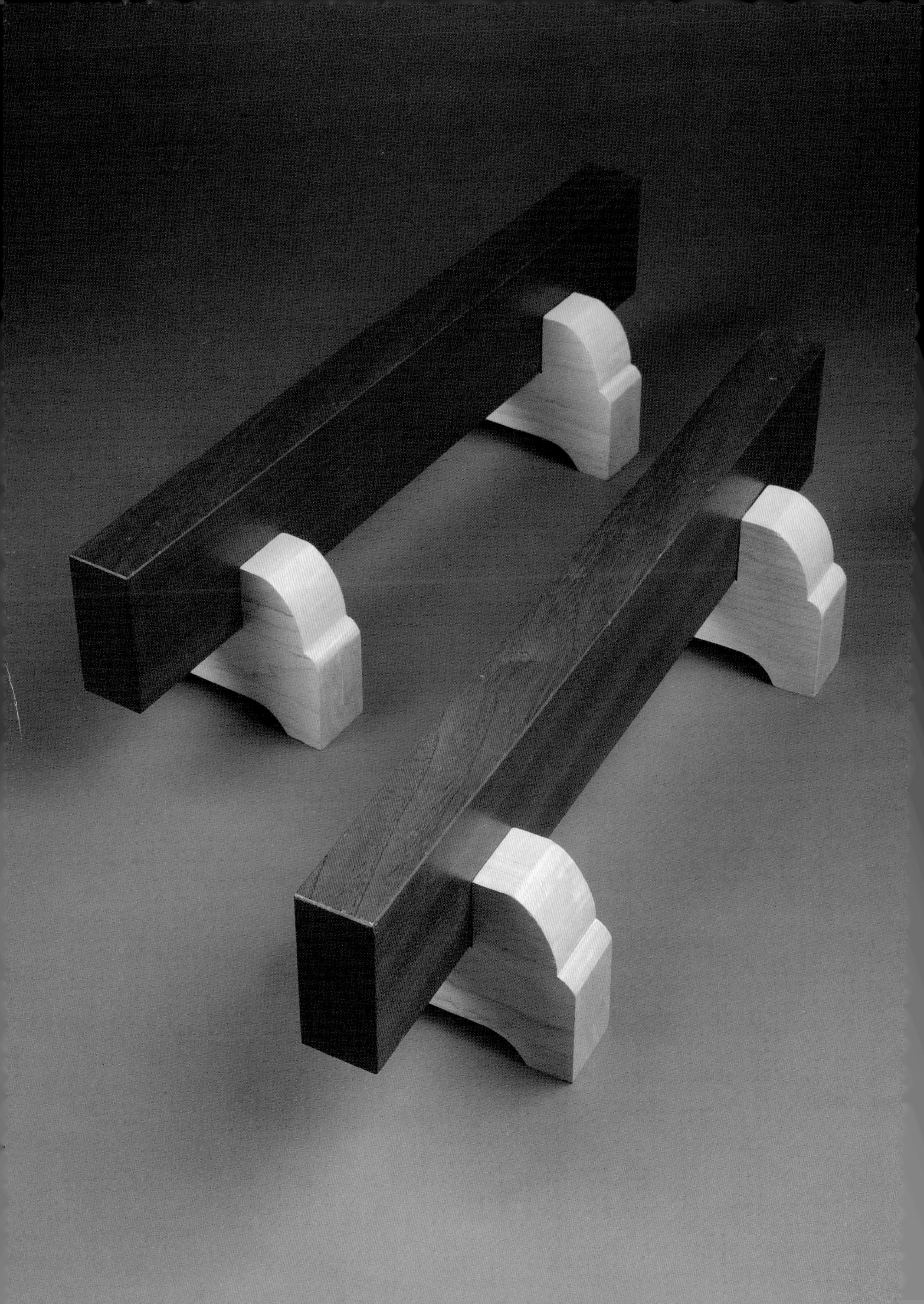

# JAPANESE WORK TRESTLES

Just as tools differ between Western and Eastern cultures, so do working practices. This is particularly true of Japan, which has a long tradition of its craftsmen working at floor level. I first made this little project from some maple offcuts and a length of sapele for an article in *Furniture & Cabinetmaking* on this subject, never thinking I would have use for such an item.

But I have since replicated the design on site more than once to create an instant working platform from scraps of softwood. The benefits don't stop on site; used on a benchtop, this pair of trestles can raise a workpiece to a more suitable height for sawing instead of hunching over the vise. The components are not glued, so the trestles can be packed away and transported easily.

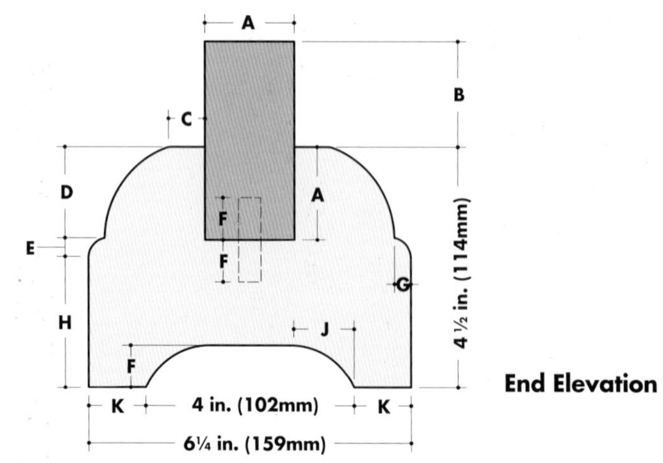


**End Elevation**

**KEY**

A = 1 3/4 in. (44mm)
B = 1 31/32 in. (50mm)
C = 11/16 in. (17mm)
D = 1 11/16 in. (43mm)
E = 3/8 in. (10mm)
F = 3/4 in. (19mm)
G = 5/16 in. (8mm)
H = 2 7/16 in. (62mm)
J = 1 3/16 in. (30mm)
K = 1 1/8 in. (29mm)
L = 3 11/16 in. (94mm)
M = 4 5/8 in. (117mm)
N = 14 1/2 in. (368mm)
P = 4 1/2 in. (114mm)
Q = 2 3/4 in. (70mm)

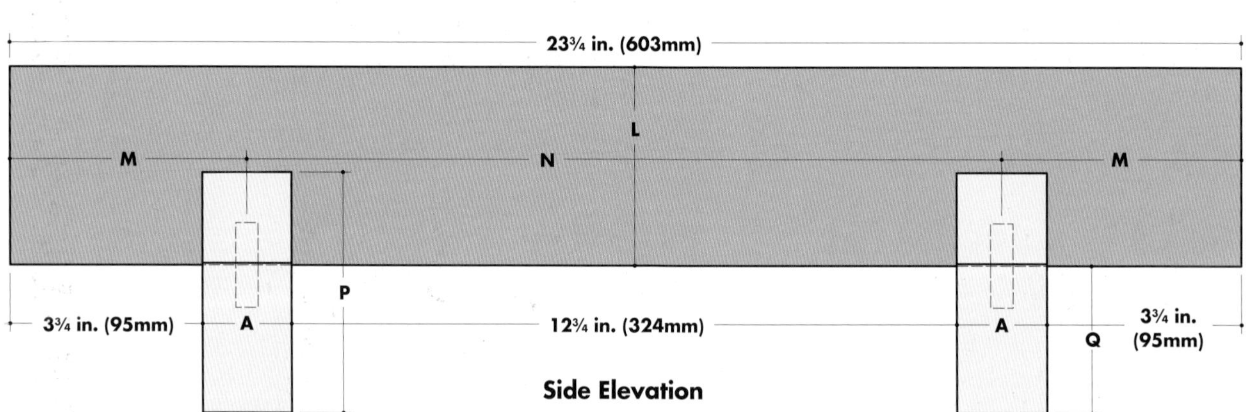


**Side Elevation**

**Exploded Diagram**

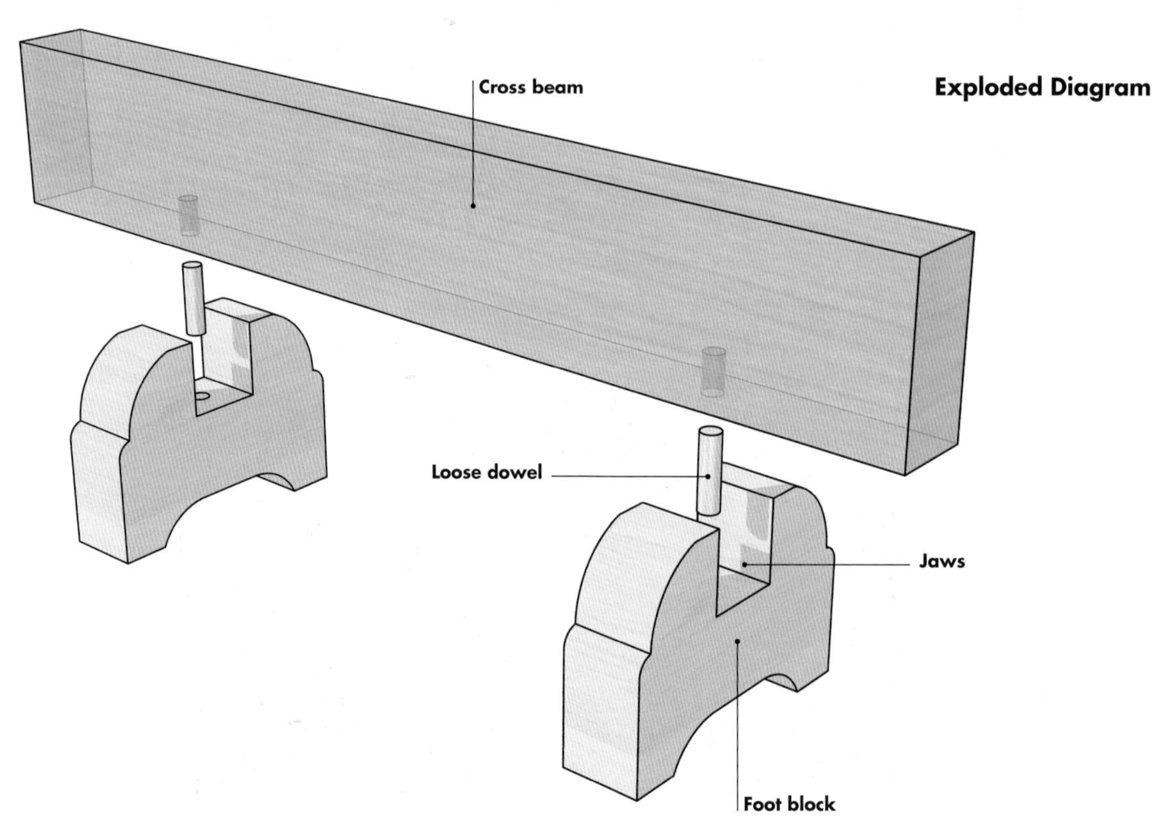

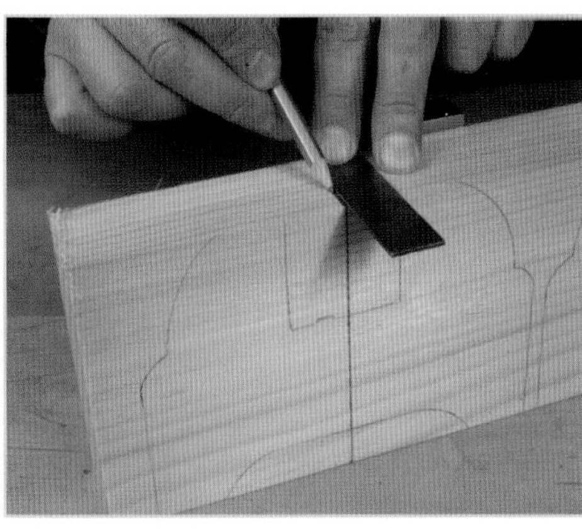

1 Start by marking out a pattern for the foot blocks. The design is not important as long as you work from a center line.

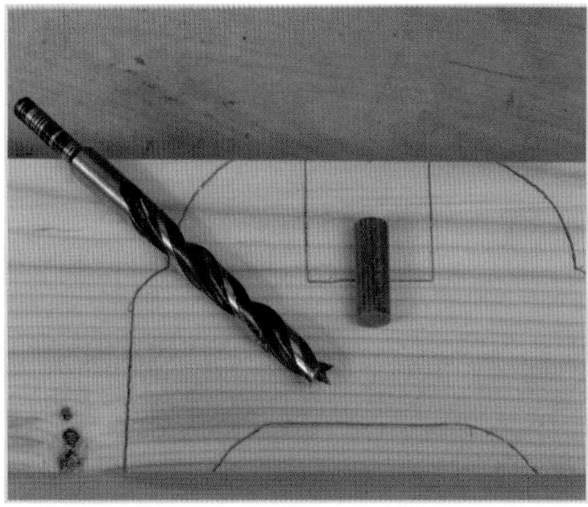

2 Select the size of dowel and match it to a drill that will allow you to bore a hole from the top of the block down between the jaws. The holes must be square in both directions.

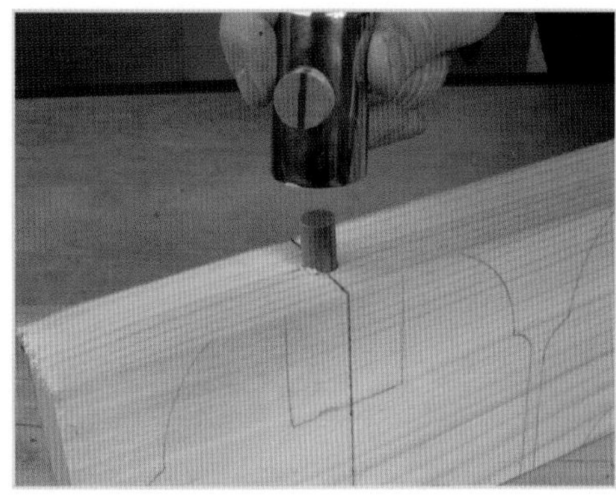

3 Cut the dowels to length and insert them halfway into the holes on the top of the block.

4 Having drilled matching holes in your beams, place them over the dowels and square them to the face of the block.

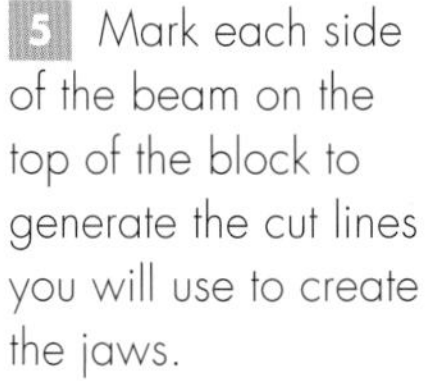

5 Mark each side of the beam on the top of the block to generate the cut lines you will use to create the jaws.

**6** If you are in the workshop and have access to a bandsaw, you can be more elaborate with your design. For shaped work you will prolong the life of your blade if you make some escape cuts down to the line before cutting the profile.

**7** Although I have a bandsaw, I still prefer to cut the jaws by hand, having transferred the lines down the face of the block from the top edge.

**8** Make a few more cuts down to the base line with the saw and chop out the waste with a chisel. Be mean with your chopping; little and often will achieve better results. Work from both faces to avoid breakout beyond the base line.

**9** A snug fit rather than a tight one is required; you may want to use a rasp to fine-tune things.

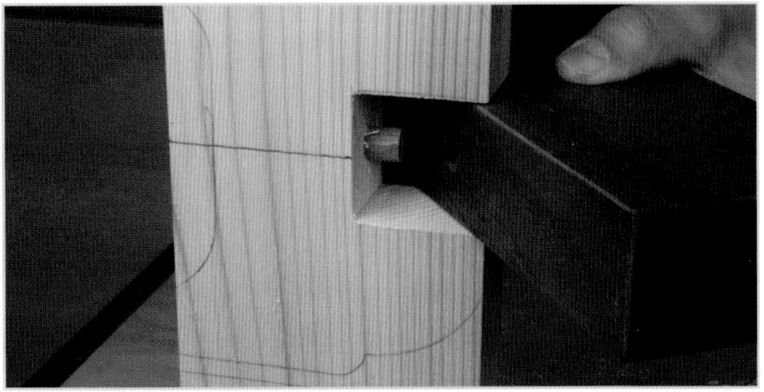

**10** Insert a dowel in the hole and test the fit with the beam.

**11** Use the rasp to tidy up the convex edges. Sand afterward if you want a smooth finish.

**12** A curved rasp can be used to clean up the concave shape at the base of the foot block.

*Your finished Japanese work trestle will look something like this. You will need to make two.*

# LETTER RACK

I like to work "off center" whenever I can, whether it be in the workshop or on site, as the center seems to be the most reliable and convenient reference for any number of measurements. Every component has a center in two axes. Once established, it can be used to unify repetitive cutting, drilling, and location. This project also uses the alignment jig described at the beginning of the book (see page 27).

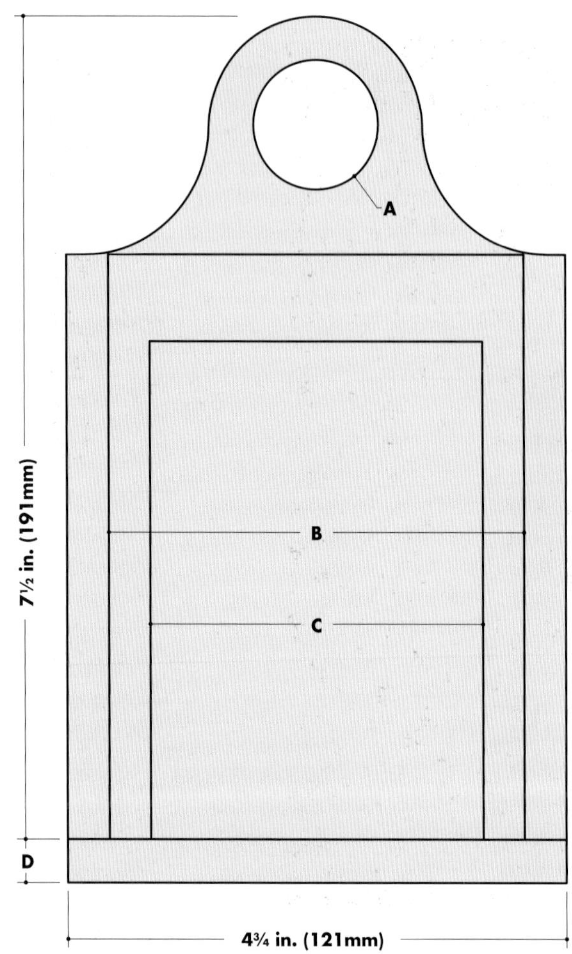


End Elevation

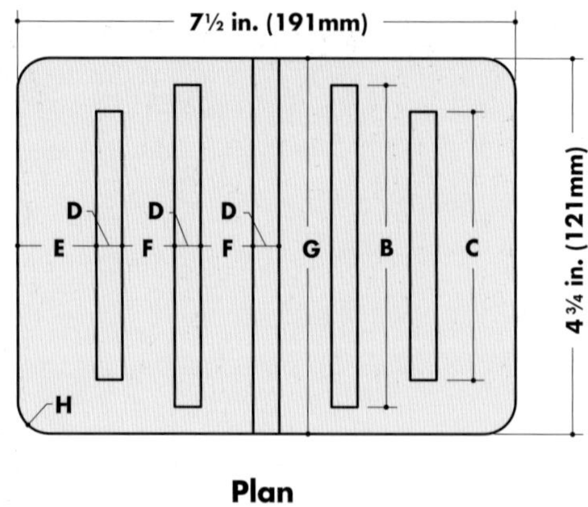


Plan

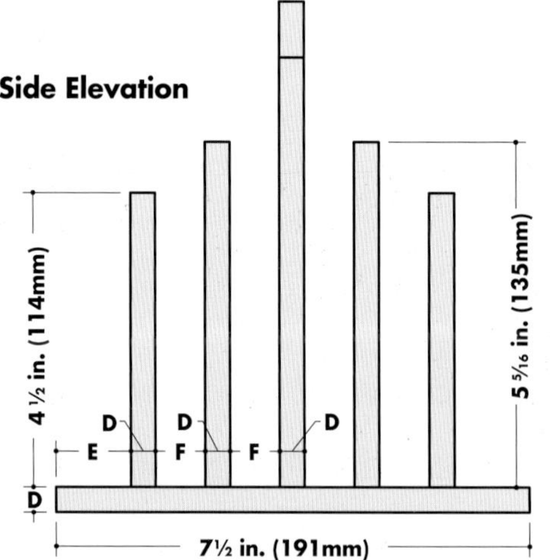


Side Elevation

**KEY**

**A = 1 3/16 in. dia. (30mm)**

**B = 4 in. (102mm)**

**C = 3 1/8 in. (80mm)**

**D = 3/8 in. (10mm)**

**E = 1 5/16 in. (33mm)**

**F = 3/4 in. (19mm)**

**G = 4 3/4 in. (121mm)**

**H = 1/2 in. (12mm) radius**

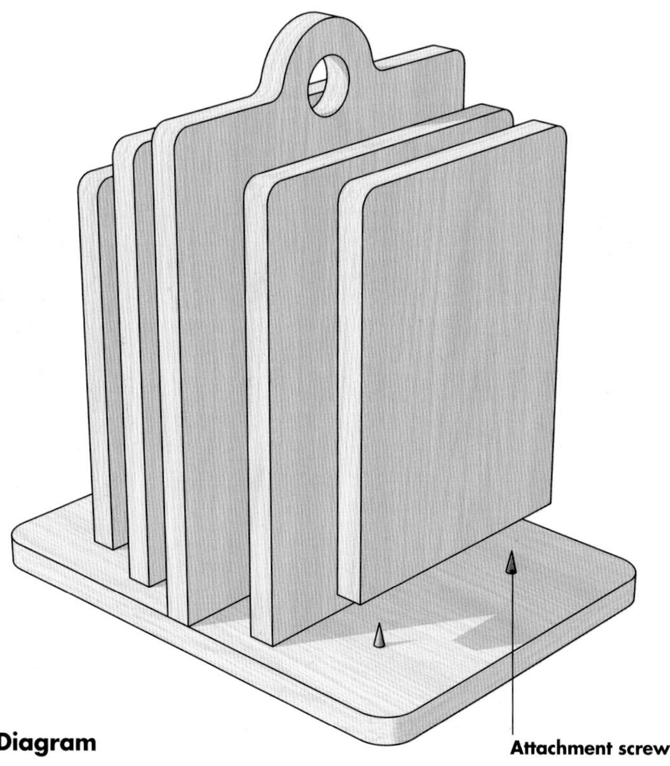


Exploded Diagram

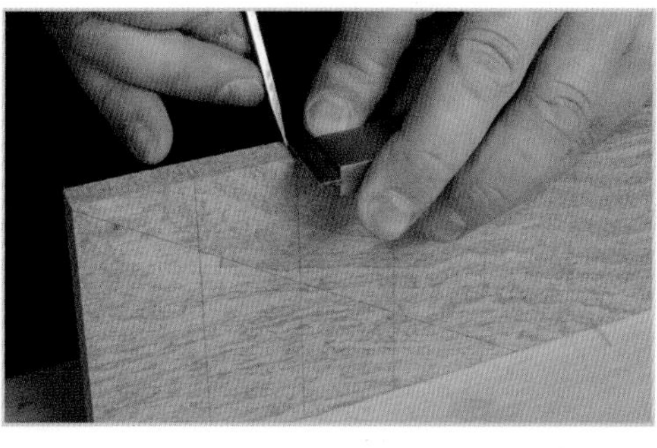

**1** On the underside of the base, find the center by scribing lines from corner to corner. Mark a centerline. Then, working from center, mark additional lines to locate the centers of the dividers—in this case 1⅛ in. (29mm) apart.

**2** Use a square to extend the lines down both edges of the base, and number each line. It can help with registration to lightly go over your scribe lines with a pencil if the components are going to be handled repeatedly.

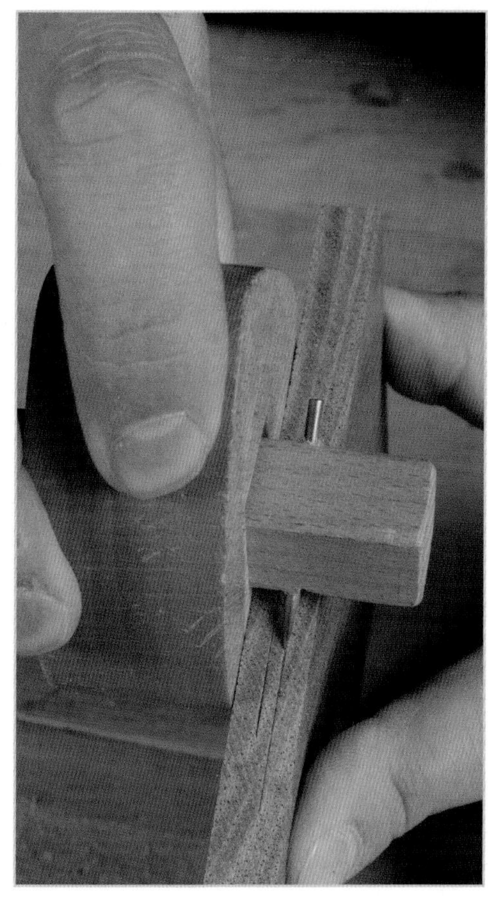

**3** Take one of the dividers; with a marking gauge, place a line clearly off-center on the bottom edge, then replicate this line from the other face.

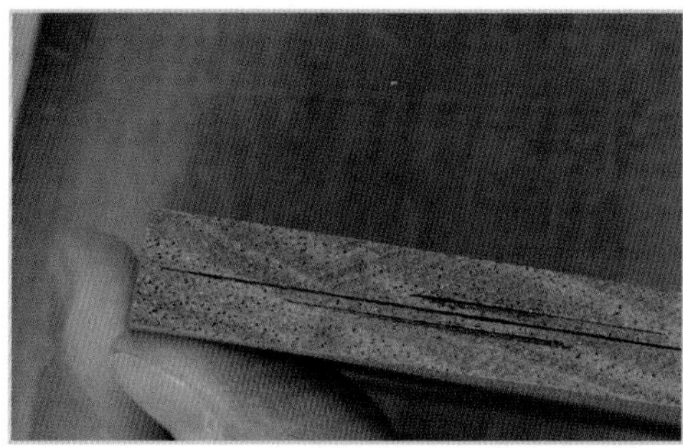

**4** It should now be simple to find the center of the piece by eye by centering the gauge point between the two marks. Just tap the rod of the gauge on the bench to make tiny adjustments without having to use a ruler. Extend the mark a short way along both sides.

**5** Begin by taking the first divider (the middle one, in this case) and clamp it to one side of the alignment box jig, tight up to the fence and flush with the top.

6 Now place the base face down on top of the jig, line up the marks up on the edge, and clamp the base in place. Number the lines and the corresponding dividers.

7 Drill through the centerline on the base into the divider with a 1/16-in. (2mm) drill bit. To avoid having to mark out an exact position for the holes, be sure to have the numbers all facing the same way as you clamp a piece into the jig. Repeat for all the dividers, keeping the pilot holes away from the edges. Now re-drill the holes in the base to the gauge of the screws—1/8 in. (3mm) in this case—and countersink.

8 A simple way to lay out the shape at the top of the middle divider is to divide the width by four. Draw a line across the board 1 3/16 in. (30mm) from the top. With a compass set to a width of 1 3/16 in., divide the line into fourths. Place the compass at the center and draw the semicircle. Reduce the compass setting by about 1/32 in. (1mm) and draw the arcs on either side of the semi-circle. You may need to feather the lines to connect them smoothly.

9 The shape can be cut using either a bandsaw or a jigsaw. Make a series of straight cuts into the curves, stopping just short of the finished line to let the waste fall away easily and prevent the blade from overheating.

10 An oscillating spindle sander will make light work of smoothing the curves, although a sheet of sandpaper wrapped around a thick piece of dowel will work just as well. To finish off, drill a 1 1/4-in. (32mm) diameter hole in the center of the top curve to serve as a finger hole.

**11** With all the holes drilled, you can now resize the uprights by cutting the same amount of material from each side. Now is the time to do any rounding of corners and sanding, and finish with a food-safe oil such as tung oil.

**12** When you assemble the letter rack, be sure the numbers on the dividers correspond with those on the base in sequence and in orientation.

*Your finished letter rack will look something like this.*

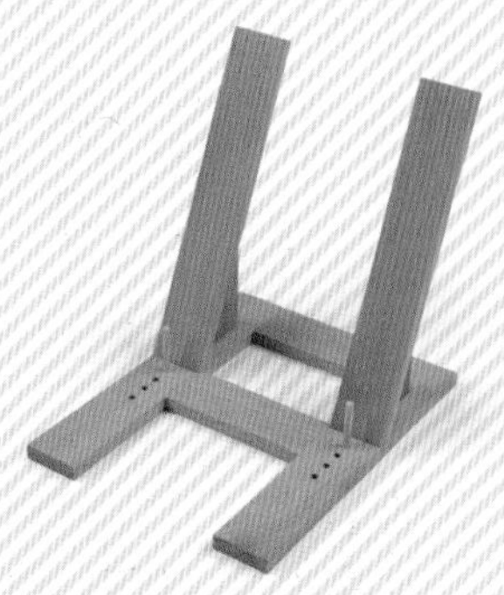

# COOKBOOK HOLDER

I've called this project a cookbook holder, but it could just as easily be used to support or display pictures. One problem with making an object designed to support other, heavier items is making sufficiently strong joints without having to use wide or thick stock.

This project uses a couple of joints, one quite traditional and the other a version of a typical mortise and tenon produced with a Festool Domino joiner. Instead, you could use a biscuit joiner or regular dowels. The frame is essentially two identical angle brackets attached to each other. The key is to match the brackets precisely.

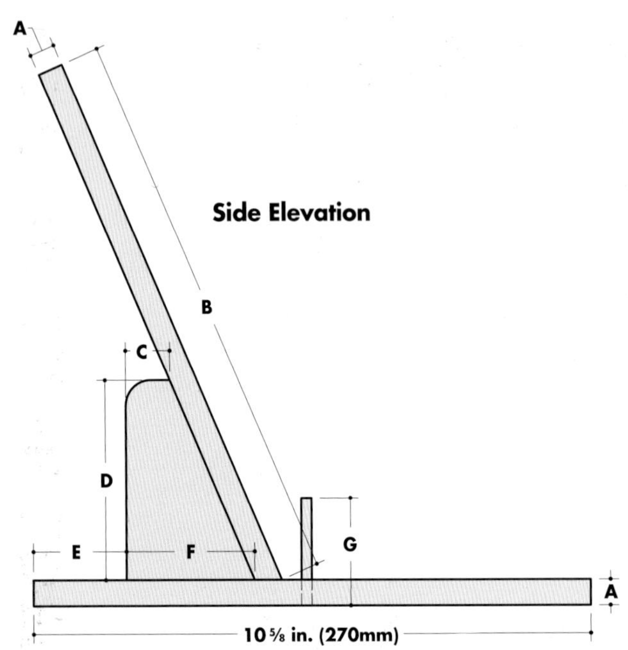

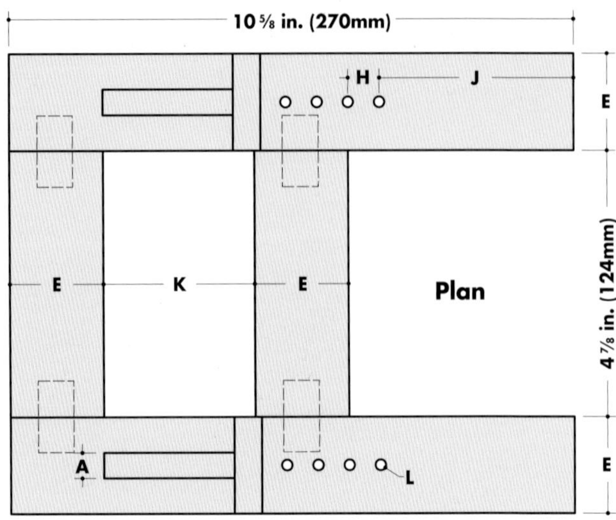

Side Elevation
A
B
C
D
E
F
G
A
10 5/8 in. (270mm)

10 5/8 in. (270mm)
H
J
E
E
K
E
Plan
4 7/8 in. (124mm)
A
L
E

**KEY**

A = $\frac{1}{2}$ in. (12mm)
B = $10\frac{5}{16}$ in. (262mm)
C = $\frac{13}{16}$ in. (21mm)
D = $3\frac{11}{16}$ in. (94mm)
E = $1\frac{3}{4}$ in. (44mm)
F = $2\frac{7}{16}$ in. (62mm)
G = 2 in. (51mm)
H = $\frac{5}{8}$ in. (16mm)
J = $3\frac{1}{2}$ in. (89mm)
K = $2\frac{7}{8}$ in. (73mm)
L = $\frac{3}{16}$ in. dia. (5mm)

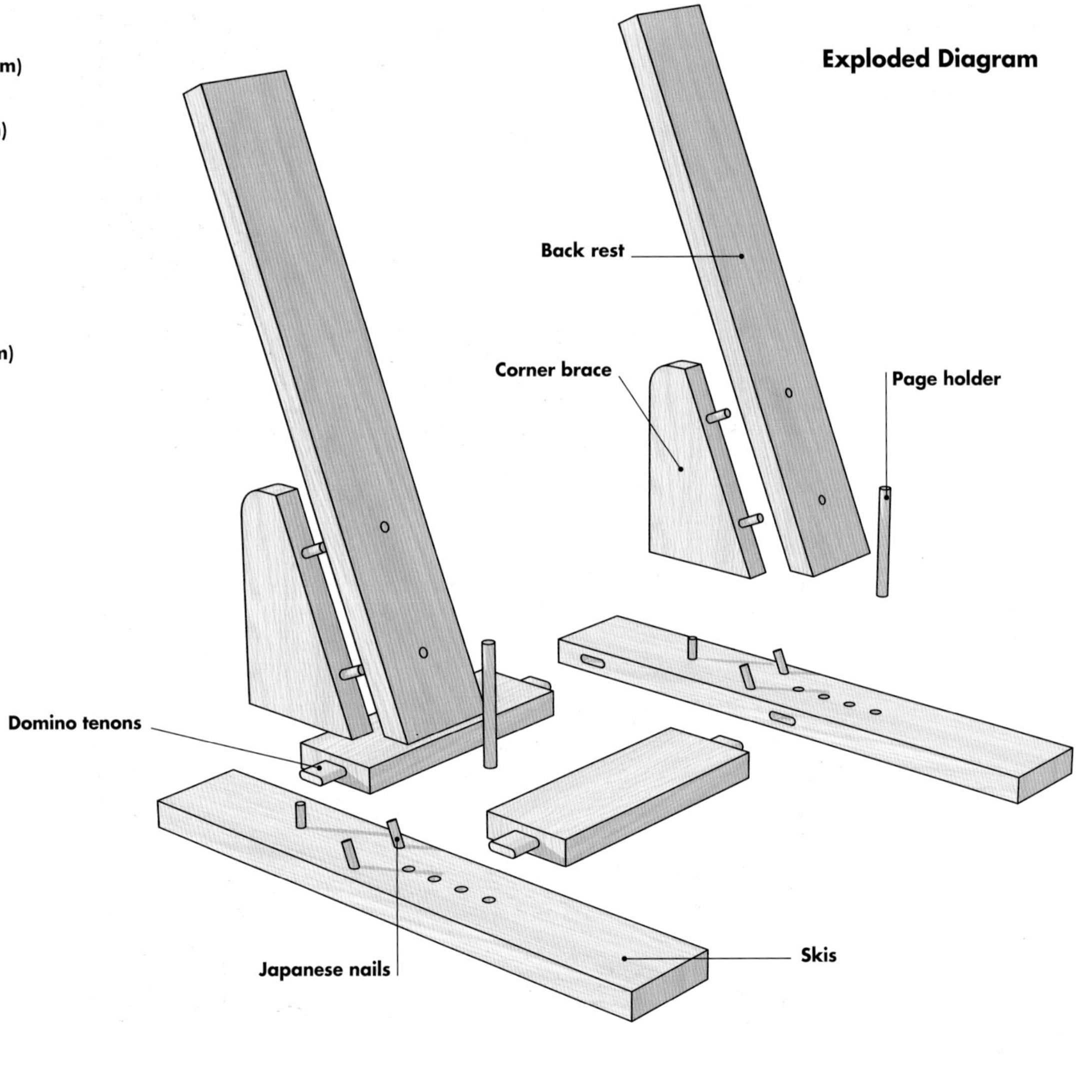

Exploded Diagram
Back rest
Corner brace
Page holder
Domino tenons
Skis
Japanese nails

1 Cut the two corner braces roughly to size and stick them together with double-sided tape, making sure the back edges are flush with each other.

2 With both of the pieces in a vise, plane the angle. The exact angle is not nearly as critical as making the components identical.

3 After shaping the top of the corner braces, mark a square line with which to create a flat bottom.

4 Set a sliding bevel to this angle...

5 ...and transfer the angle to the bottom edge of the back rest pieces.

6 Separate the corner braces and apply double-sided tape to the sloping edge.

7 With center lines marked on the corner braces and back rests, place the corner braces firmly in position.

8 Japanese wooden nails are tapered and require a tapered drill bit to drill a pilot hole. Set the depth of the hole by winding masking tape around the drill bit. If you can't locate wooden nails, try Miller dowels instead.

9 Drill through the face of the book rest into the corner brace, then trim the end of the rest to match the bottom of the corner brace.

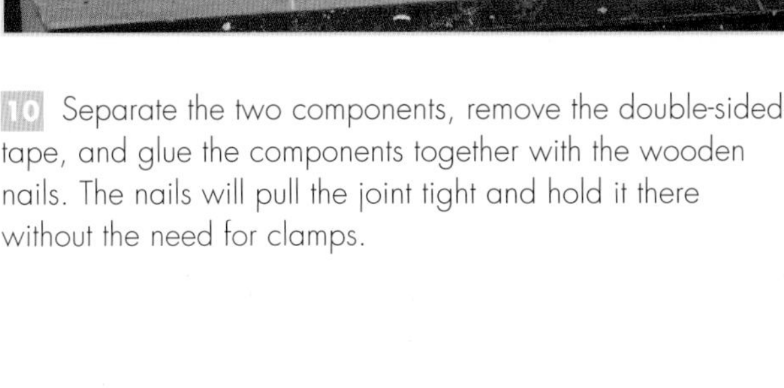

**10** Separate the two components, remove the double-sided tape, and glue the components together with the wooden nails. The nails will pull the joint tight and hold it there without the need for clamps.

**11** Repeat the process to attach the book rest arms to the skis. Mark the angle of the drill to help guide you, but don't glue the pieces together at this point.

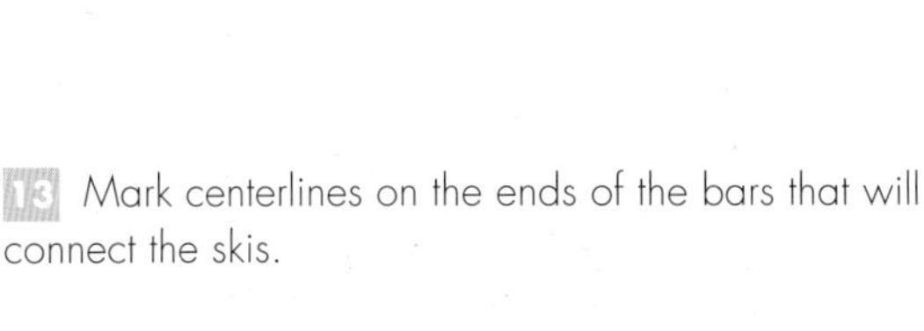

**12** With the rests attached to the skis, set them side by side and prepare to cut the skis to length.

**13** Mark centerlines on the ends of the bars that will connect the skis.

14 Transfer these marks to the skis.

15 The bit for the Domino machine needs to be set to cut its hole in the center of the stock.

16 If the stock thickness is less than the minimum setting on the machine, use a thin piece of scrap to raise it off the benchtop to the required height.

17 The Domino jointer can be set to cut mortises or slots wider than the tenon insert, allowing some lateral adjustment when it comes to final assembly.

18 Cut slots for all the joints in the skis and crossbars.

19 Drill peg holes in the skis in front of the book rest and glue the frame together.

20 Sand the joints of the frame flush and attach the book rests using the Japanese wooden nails.

*Your finished cookbook holder will look something like this.*

# BIRDHOUSE

At first glance, this birdhouse looks fairly straightforward to make. However, I have introduced a less-than-standard angle (80°) to create the pitch to the roof so you can practice planing an edge to a board that is not square. If you want to simplify things, adjust the angle to 90° and use a combination square to mark the roof line.

I have a few of these birdhouses in my garden; they get used every year, reminding me that sometimes the simplest projects can be the most rewarding. The measurements are fairly critical; if you are building a box with a particular species in mind, check with your local wildlife organization for the appropriate size of entry hole and height from the base of the box.

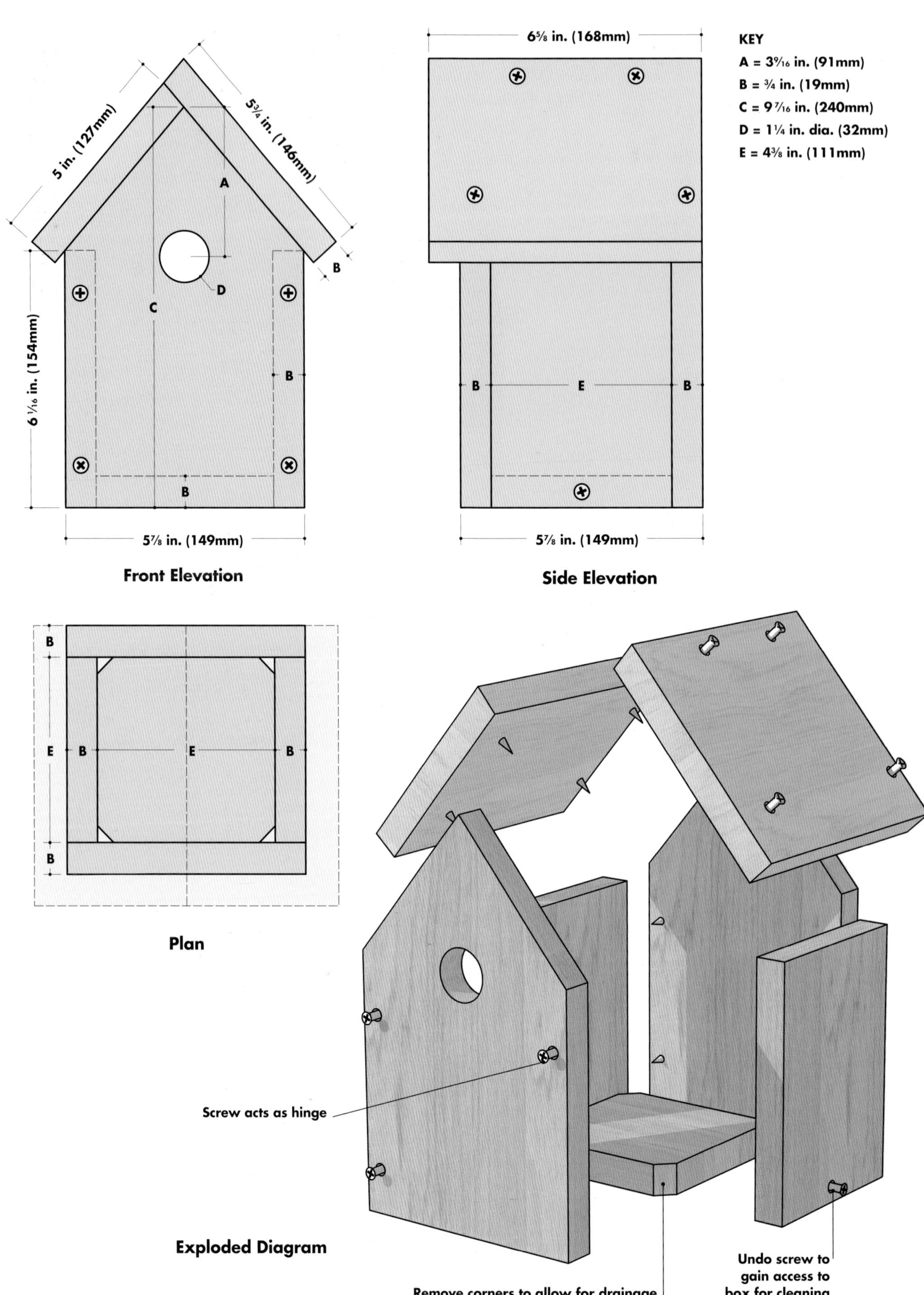
6⅝ in. (168mm)
KEY
A = 3⁹⁄₁₆ in. (91mm)
B = ¾ in. (19mm)
C = 9⁷⁄₁₆ in. (240mm)
D = 1¼ in. dia. (32mm)
E = 4⅜ in. (111mm)
5 in. (127mm)
5¾ in. (146mm)
A
B
D
C
6¹⁄₁₆ in. (154mm)
B
B
5⅞ in. (149mm)
Front Elevation
B
E
B
5⅞ in. (149mm)
Side Elevation
B
E
B
E
B
B
Plan
Screw acts as hinge
Exploded Diagram
Remove corners to allow for drainage
Undo screw to gain access to box for cleaning

1 Take your offcut and mark the length of the front and back panels.

2 Set your sliding bevel to 130°. Mark diagonal lines from the middle of the board to the edges to create the pitch of the roof.

3 Mark the center of the entry hole.

4 Drill the hole. If you have enough material, it is not much more work to make these in pairs; you could even make an extra front to use as a template next time.

**5** Set the board in a vise, using a square to position the guidelines vertically.

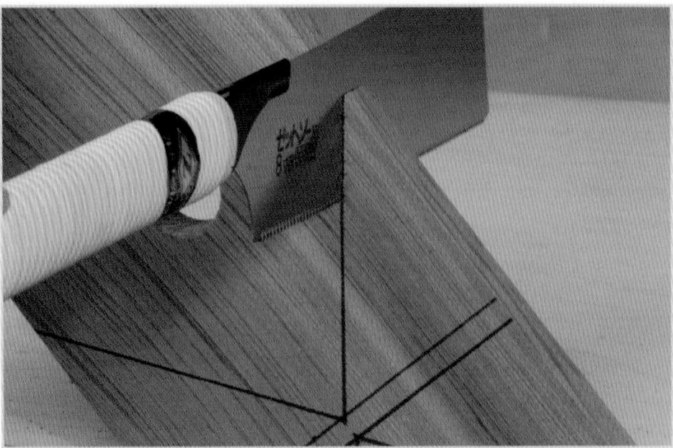

**6** Saw the components, rotating the block each time you complete a cut.

**7** On a second board, use the front as a template to mark the back panel.

**8** Cut the back panel in the same way as the front and match the pair.

**9** Place both panels in a vise with sides and bottom edges flush and plane the angled edges so they are level and the same size as each other.

**10** Cut the sides and bottom. Remove the corners of the bottom to provide drainage holes if the box ever takes on water.

**11** Clamp the components together and drill holes for screws.

**12** Pilot holes will ensure that you won't split any of the components when you assemble them.

**13** Set the sliding bevel to the pitch of the roof. It should be 80°, but don't worry if it is a little off.

**14** Cut the roof pieces oversize and transfer the angle to the ends of each piece. Plane the edges to match the angle, checking against the roof to make sure that they meet without any gaps.

**15** Screw the roof in place and mark off the end of the long side from the one on the opposite side.

**16** Square off this line and cut the roof piece to match the other side.

*Your finished birdhouse will look something like this.*

# GARDEN PLANTER

When making anything for use outside, select a material that is fit for that purpose. This garden planter is made from iroko, a relative of ash. It may be hard to find in the U.S., but wenge, beech, and paulownia are among the alternatives. I made this iroko planter from leftover decking material; it requires the minimum of finish for it to withstand all that the elements can throw at it before deteriorating beyond repair.

The joinery in this project is not technically challenging, but an element of precise hand tool coordination is required for the finishing touches. A router table would make life easier, but is not essential.

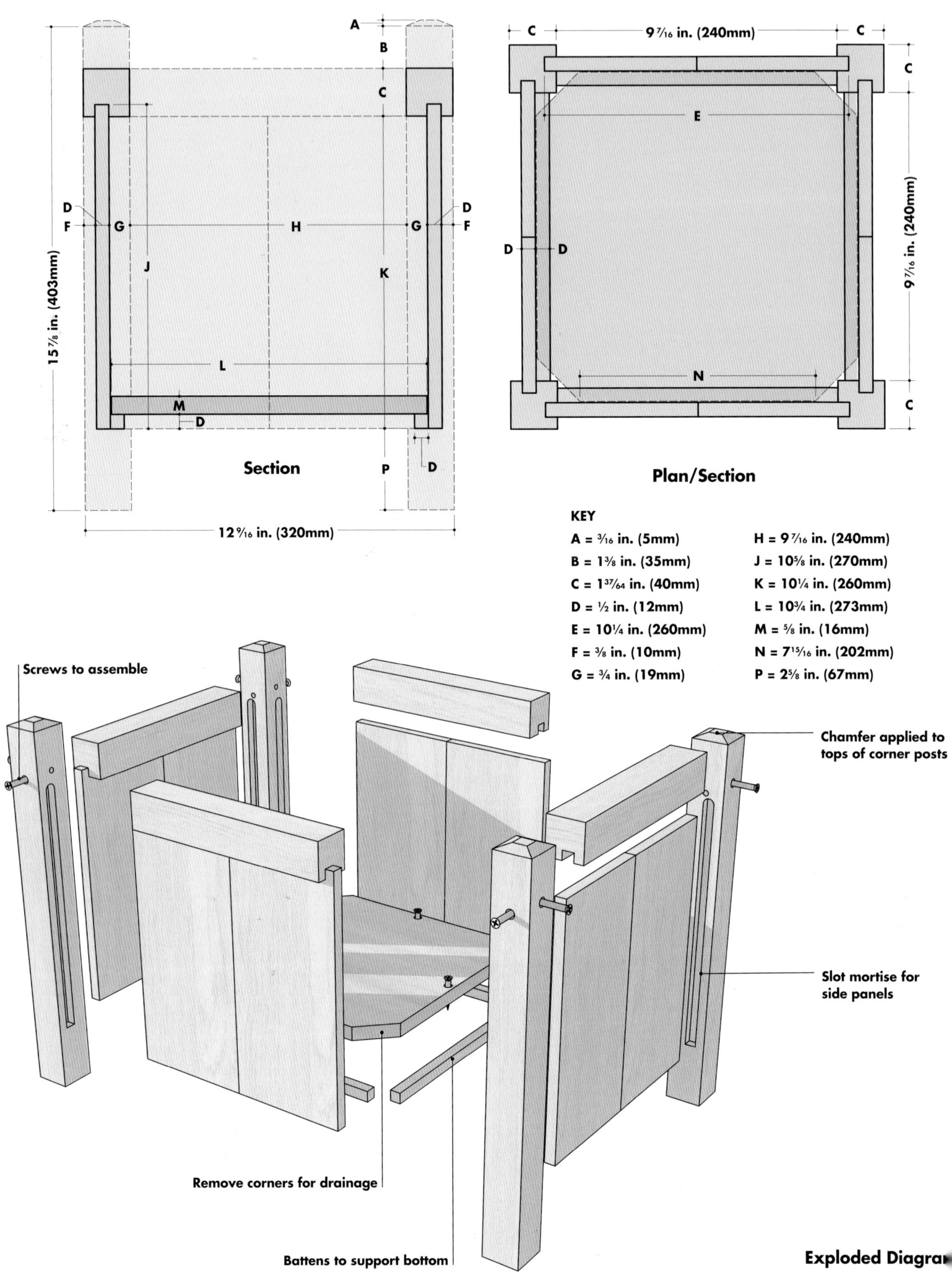

A
B
C
D
F
G
H
J
K
L
M
P
15 7/8 in. (403mm)
12 9/16 in. (320mm)
Section
9 7/16 in. (240mm)
E
N
Plan/Section
KEY
A = 3/16 in. (5mm)
B = 1 3/8 in. (35mm)
C = 1 37/64 in. (40mm)
D = 1/2 in. (12mm)
E = 10 1/4 in. (260mm)
F = 3/8 in. (10mm)
G = 3/4 in. (19mm)
H = 9 7/16 in. (240mm)
J = 10 5/8 in. (270mm)
K = 10 1/4 in. (260mm)
L = 10 3/4 in. (273mm)
M = 5/8 in. (16mm)
N = 7 15/16 in. (202mm)
P = 2 5/8 in. (67mm)
Screws to assemble
Chamfer applied to tops of corner posts
Slot mortise for side panels
Remove corners for drainage
Battens to support bottom
Exploded Diagra

**1** Start by clamping a pair of legs together and laying out the position of the grooves that accept the side panels. Because the two internal faces are to be grooved, you will want to position them away from the centerline. The X-shape illustrates the position of the top rails, which are also grooved for the side panels.

**2** Attach a stop or clamp to the upper portion of the leg, to limit the amount of travel of the router when machining the grooves. If your material allows it, machine the components in pairs.

**3** I used a ½-in. (12mm) bit to match the thickness of the side panel. Using a square, measure from the tip of the bit to the outside edge of the router base. (See photo at step 2.) Transfer that dimension to the leg, shown above.

4 Use a chisel to make a clean mark across the two boards so that they can be realigned when rotated 90° to rout the second face.

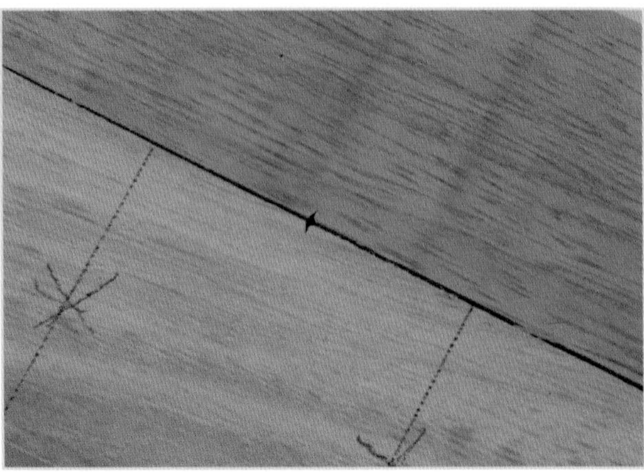

5 Line up the chisel indents. The lines marked with an 'X' are the stop lines. There is no need to mark out for the second row of grooves.

6 Square off the ends of the grooves because there is no shoulder on the panels to hide the ends.

7 Dry-clamp the frame together with the panels in place and mark locations for the screws. Avoid drilling into the groove and panels.

8 Use a strip of masking tape to set the depth of the screw hole in the corner posts.

10 On the inside of the panels, screw a batten along the bottom edge between the corner posts.

9 Because you are drilling close to the edge and into a hardwood, carry out a few tests to establish the right size of pilot hole for your screws.

11 Before assembling the frame, mark the chamfer detail on the top of the corner posts. Use a marking gauge to divide the end of the post into an even pattern.

12 With your sliding bevel set to 20°, mark the chamfer on all corners around the post.

13 You should be able to cut close to the line with a saw to remove most of the waste.

14 Fine trimming can be done with a block plane. It might help to clamp two posts together in a vise to give a more stable working platform.

15 Countersink the screw holes and screw the frame together.

16 Cut a piece of marine-grade plywood to fit in the bottom of the planter; remove the corners for drainage. Screw it to the four battens on the bottom of the sides.

*Your finished garden planter will look something like this.*

# TOOL CADDY

I have a soft spot for these tool caddies, even though I don't use one myself. It was the first project I made with my daughter when she was about six; after a short spell as a portable toy box it has now taken up residence in a cupboard under the stairs loaded with tools for impromptu DIY projects.

I pushed the boat out with this design, incorporating dovetails and a threaded handle. (You'll need a box-threading kit for the latter.) Neither feature is strictly necessary, but together they add a little twist to what is a generally utilitarian object. I haven't spent too long describing the process of dovetailing, as there are plenty of talented craftspeople who have made a career out of demonstrating this technique already.

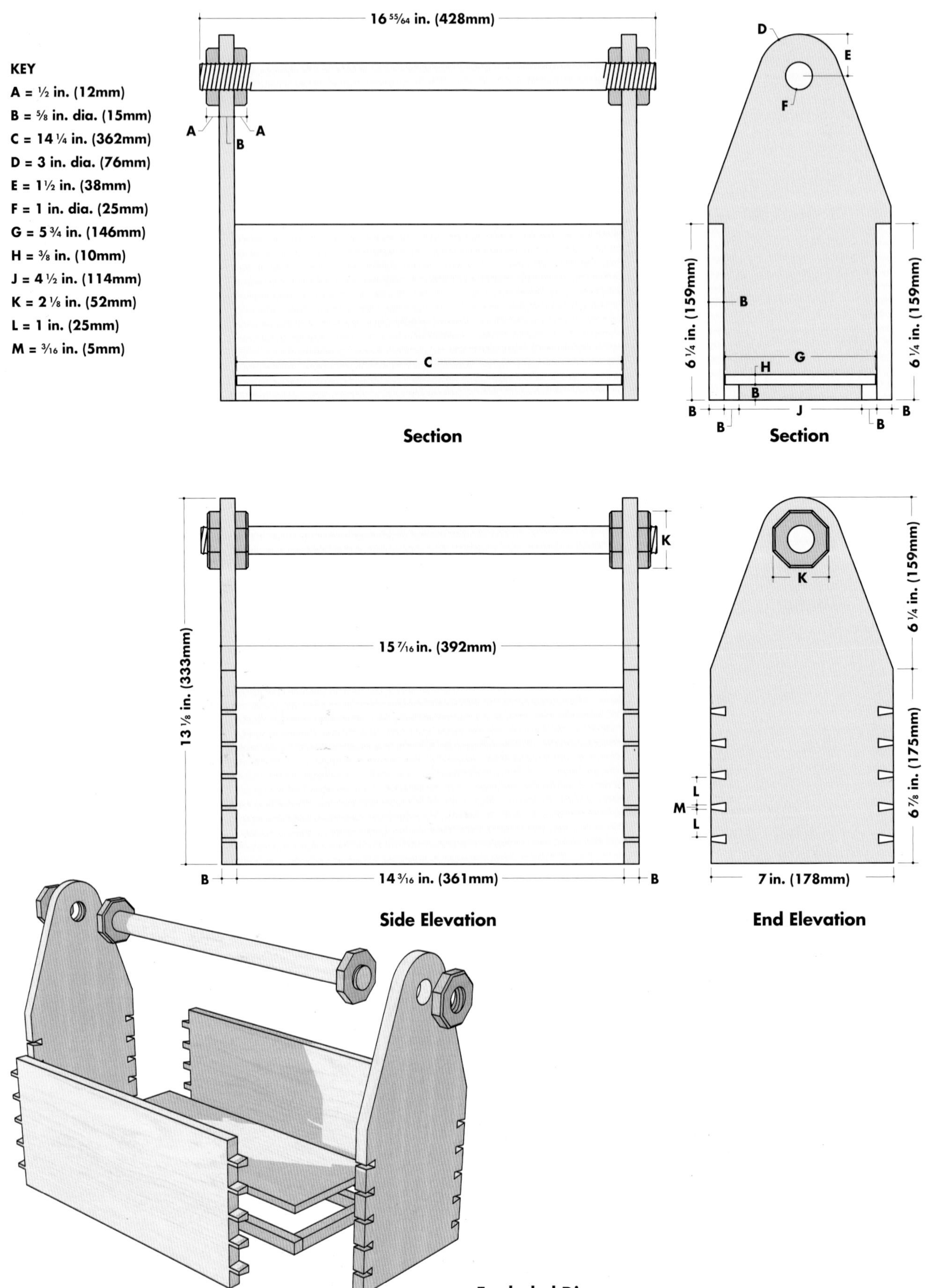
KEY
A = ½ in. (12mm)
B = ⅝ in. dia. (15mm)
C = 14 ¼ in. (362mm)
D = 3 in. dia. (76mm)
E = 1½ in. (38mm)
F = 1 in. dia. (25mm)
G = 5 ¾ in. (146mm)
H = ⅜ in. (10mm)
J = 4 ½ in. (114mm)
K = 2 ⅛ in. (52mm)
L = 1 in. (25mm)
M = 3/16 in. (5mm)
16 55/64 in. (428mm)
Section
6 ¼ in. (159mm)
Section
13 ⅛ in. (333mm)
15 7/16 in. (392mm)
14 3/16 in. (361mm)
Side Elevation
6 ⅞ in. (175mm)
7 in. (178mm)
End Elevation
Exploded Diagram

1 Start by cutting and shaping one of the ends to its finished dimensions. Place some double-sided tape around the edges.

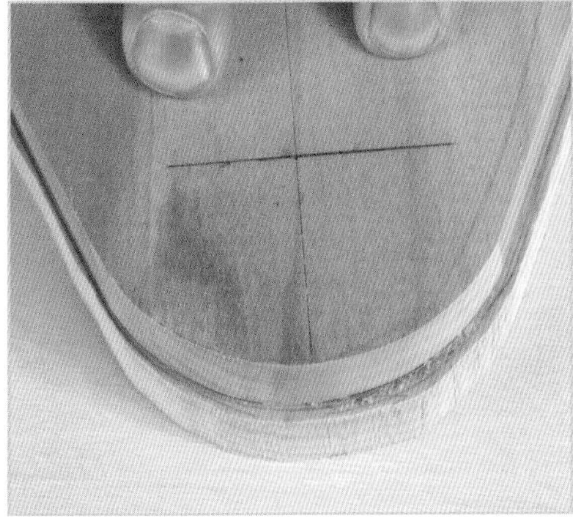

2 Cut the second end piece slightly oversize. Attach it to the first piece and mark a center point for the bar handle.

3 Using a bottom-flush-trim router bit, machine the components on a router table or benchtop to achieve a matched pair. Drill the hole for the handle.

4 Set a wheel or marking gauge to the thickness of the caddy sides.

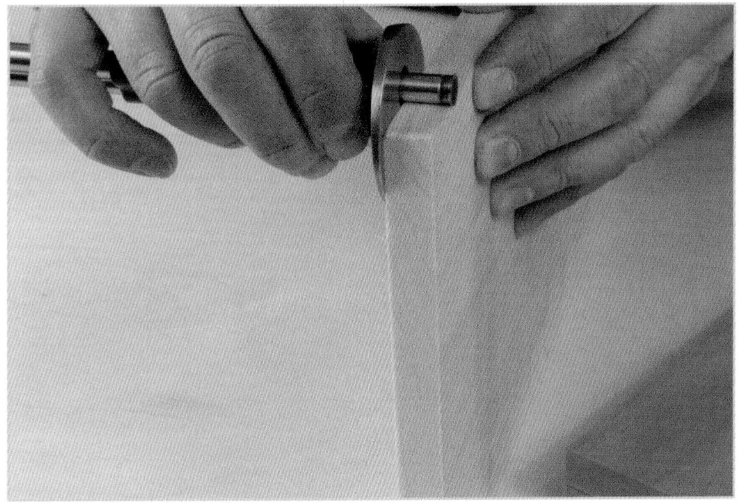

5 Transfer this dimension to both faces of the stacked end pieces; this mark is a base line for the pins.

6 Along one edge, mark out the centerlines for a row of dovetails.

7 Use a square to transfer these marks to the opposite side and carry the lines down the edge of the stack.

8 While the two ends are still attached, cut the sockets for the pins to create the tails. You can work from both sides of the stack as long as the saw cuts don't go beyond the base line.

9 With a fret saw, remove the waste in between the tails. Leave a tiny amount to chop out with a sharp chisel later.

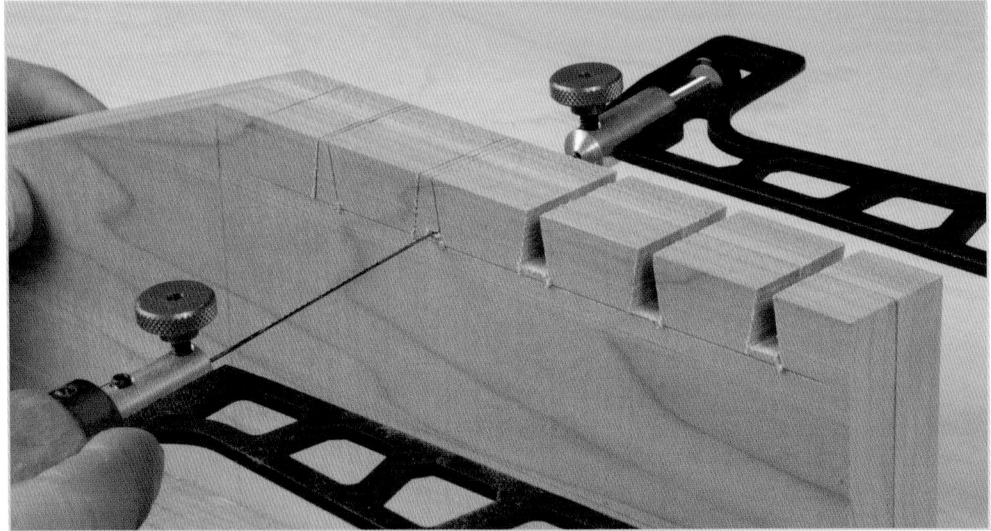

**10** Finish the sockets by chopping down to the base line with a chisel, keeping the sides in the stack.

**11** Separate the sides. Use your alignment jig (see page 27) to clamp the ends and sides in place to mark the pins. Take this opportunity to mark the components so you can keep them in the correct orientation.

**12** It is a good idea to mark out the waste material at this point, clearly identifying the pins before making any cuts.

**13** Use the fret saw to remove the waste between the pins; as before, cut shy of the base line.

**14** Trim the pins and base line with a chisel, cutting across the pins, not down them. Because the direction of the grain on the end pieces is perpendicular to that of the sides, do not attempt a tight fit.

**15** On a scrap of hardwood, mark out a square with a cross to establish the center.

**16** Set your dividers to draw a circle within the square and scribe an arc crossing the diagonals.

**17** Using a combination square, strike a line at 45° where the arc crosses the diagonals to create an octagon. Drill a hole about ⅛ in. (3mm) smaller in diameter than the carrying handle. Follow the instructions with your box-threading kit for the proper dimension.

**18** Box-threading kits are typically available with taps to create the thread used on the nut.

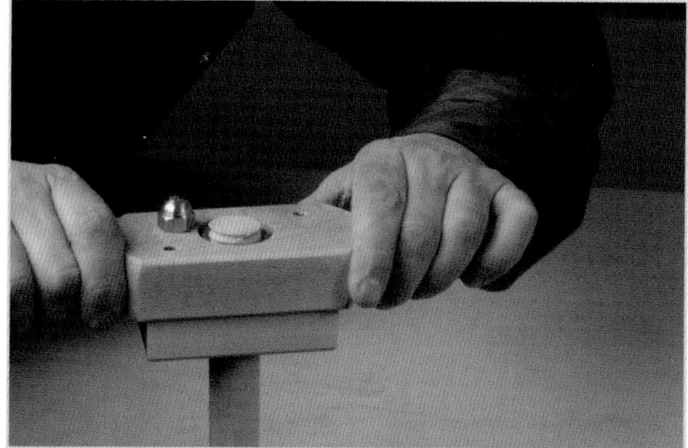

**19** Use the corresponding box-thread cutter to cut a thread on both ends of the carrying handle. Cut the threads in a single operation.

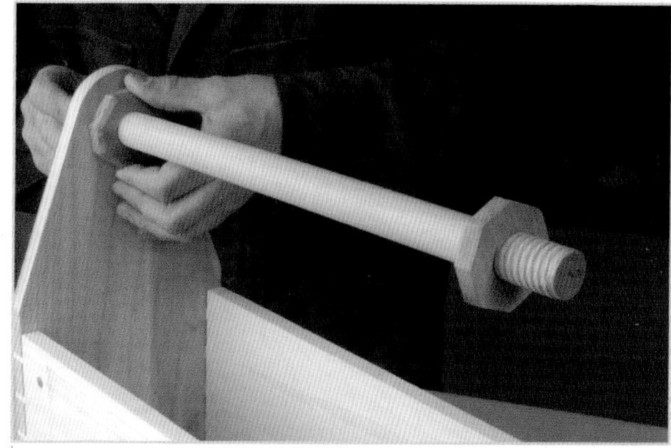

**20** Cut and shape the nuts and screw one on each end of the carrying handle.

**21** Glue the caddy together with the carrying handle in place.

**22** Use a clamping caul with cutouts to clear the pins and distribute even pressure across the dovetails.

**23** Glue and clamp battens around the base of the caddy to form a seat for the bottom piece.

**24** Adjust the nuts so that the handle fits tightly between the ends and drop a loose bottom into the caddy.

*Your finished tool caddy will look something like this.*

# DESK LAMP

Thanks to the Disney Pixar animation studio, the Luxo lamp now has a personality to go with its skeletal framework. And, just like a skeleton, the joints on this lamp are all on display. If you have completed most of the projects in this book, you should be well equipped to take on this task. The project covers only the arm, shade, and base, not the electrical components. Before you try to install the receptacle for the bulb and the wiring, I strongly urge you to consult with a licensed electrician to be sure you handle that part of the project safely.

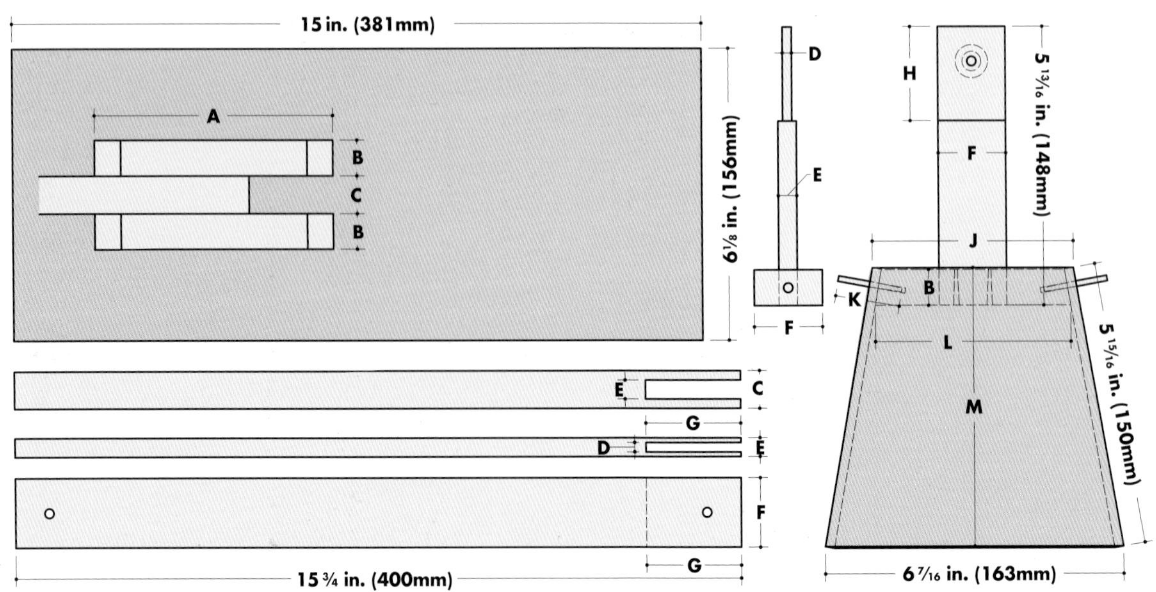


**Component Details**

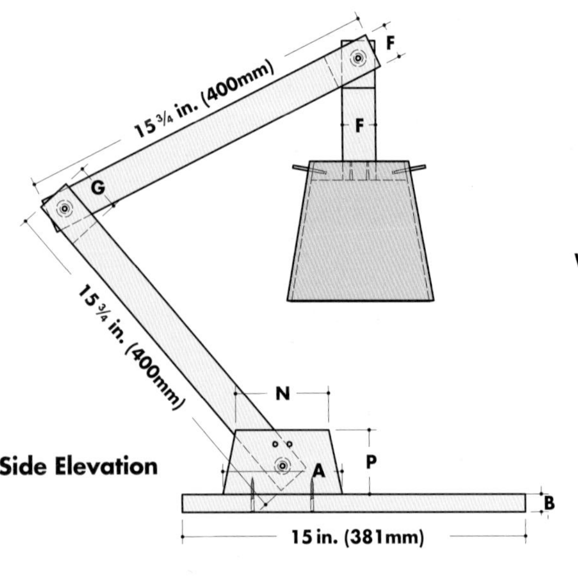


**Side Elevation**

**KEY**

A = 5³⁄₁₆ in. (132mm)
B = ¾ in. (19mm)
C = ¾ in. (19mm)
D = ³⁄₁₆ in. (5mm)
E = ⅜ in. (10mm)
F = 1½ in. (38mm)
G = 2⅛ in. (54mm)
H = 2 in. (51mm)
J = 4⁵⁄₁₆ in. (110mm)
K = 1⅜ in. (35mm)
L = 4¼ in. (108mm)
M = 5¹³⁄₁₆ in. (148mm)
N = 4¹⁄₁₆ in. (103mm)
P = 2⅝ in. (67mm)

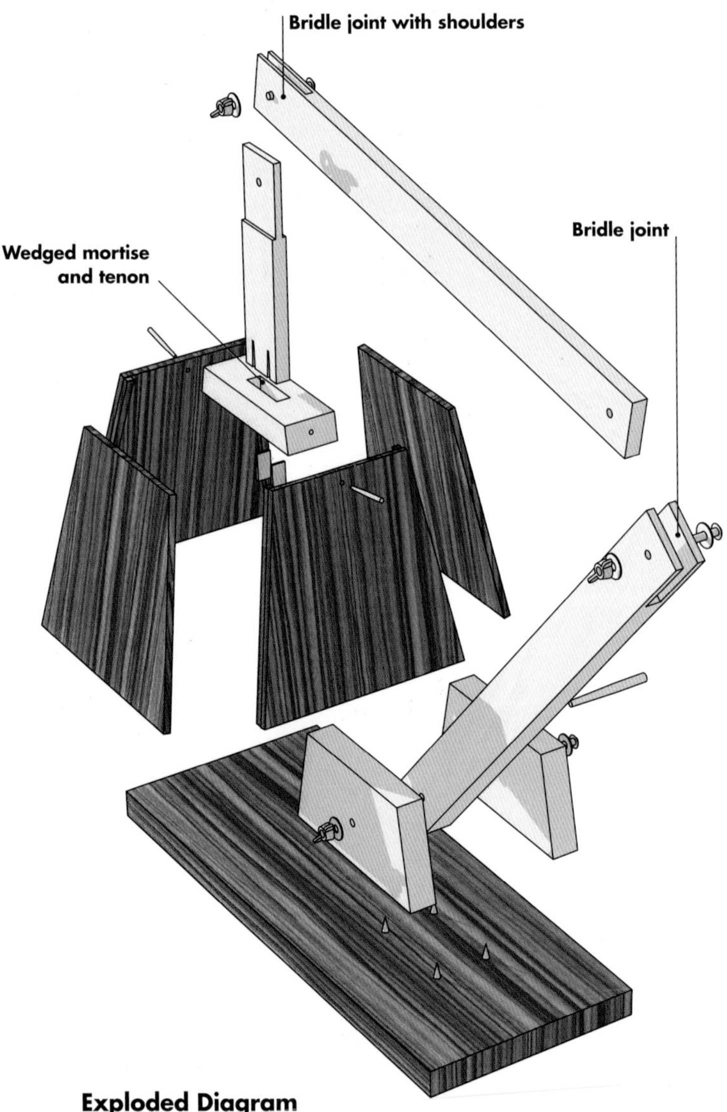


**Exploded Diagram**

1 The first joint you will need to cut is one of the two bridle joints that are used to connect the components making up the arm. Starting with the larger one first, cut the open mortise on the first section of the joint to the thickness of the middle one.

2 Drill a hole at the bottom of the mortise and chop out the waste with a chisel. Remember to work a couple of millimeters away from the base line and from both sides before completing the joint.

3 The mortise needs to be a clean fit. One way to achieve that is to thickness the mating piece after cutting the mortise.

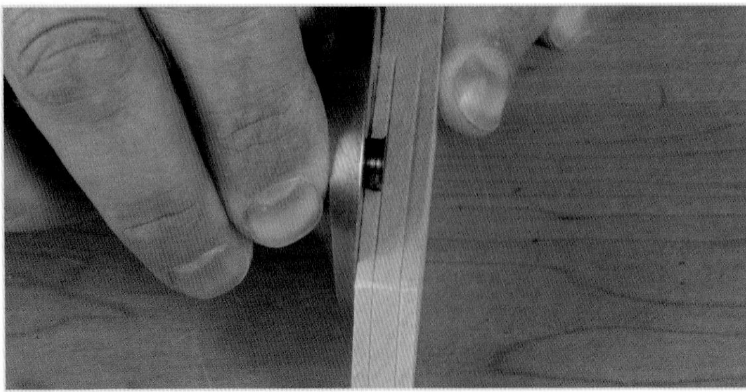

4 For the second bridle joint, you will create both parts – the open mortise and the tenon—from scratch. Divide one end of the last section.

5 Cut the shoulder lines first, stopping a blade's thickness short of the line.

6 Cut the cheeks down to the shoulder line where the waste should fall away. It is a good idea to create the tenon slightly thicker than it needs to be.

7 Use a shoulder plane to obtain a flat surface on both faces, working down to the line.

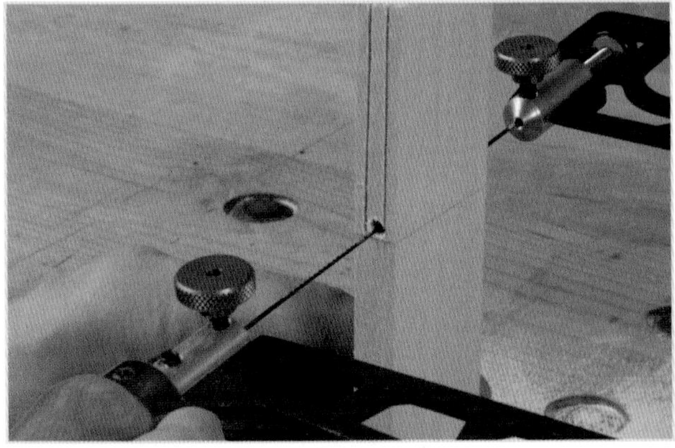

8 Using the tenon, mark the lines on one end of the middle section to cut the second open mortise. Use a fret saw to remove the waste. The block of waste can be used to level off the bottom of the mortise by wrapping a piece of sandpaper around it. Be careful not to round over the inside face of the mortise.

**9** The end of the arm is attached to a block onto which the shade is suspended. Mark around the end of the last arm component to cut a through-mortise. Remove most of the waste with a drill and chisel out the remainder.

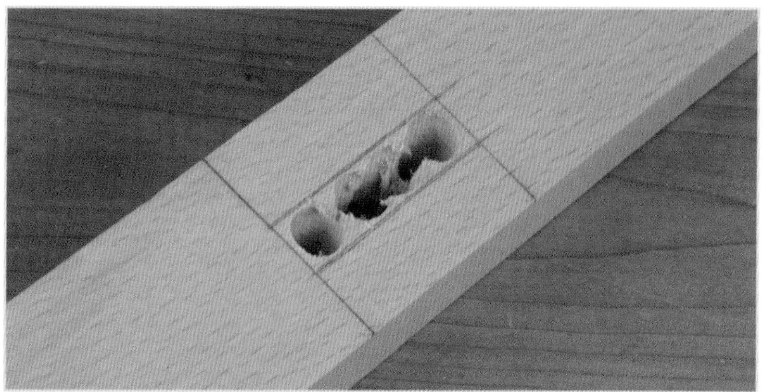

**10** This tenon does not have a shoulder, so the fit needs to be tight. When you are satisfied, take a few shavings from one edge to create a gap of around 1⁄32 in. (1mm) at each end of the tenon.

**11** Mark a line about 3⁄16 in. (5mm) up from where the shoulder line would be and drill two 1⁄8-in. (3mm) holes equidistant from the edge.

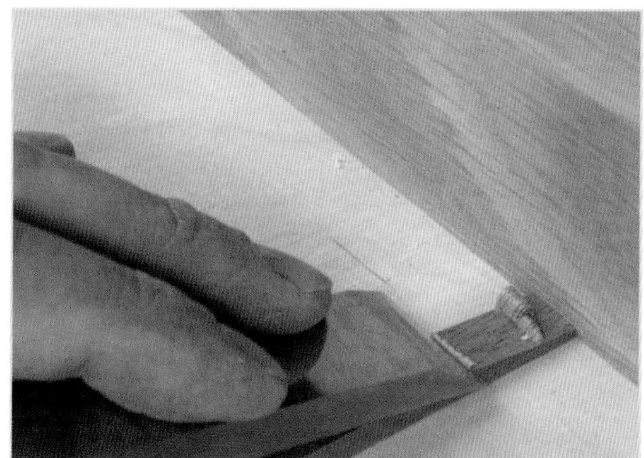

**12** Make saw cuts straight down the tenon to meet the holes. With a chisel, make two wedges that will fit the saw cut without force to about a third of its depth. Cut the block to length with 10° angles on the ends.

**13** Attach the block to the arm component by driving the wedges into the saw cuts. To achieve even spacing, tap the wedges in by equal amounts in turn until the joint is tight. It will help to mount the tenon in a vise with a block positioned to the correct depth and set square.

14 Mark centerlines on the block on all four sides and on two of the shade components. Align the marks and scribe the angle from the block onto the shade. Extend the lines with a sliding bevel, then cut and trim both pieces to match.

15 Clamp the two shade pieces to the angled ends of the block, using the centerlines for location. Do not use any glue.

16 Rest the assembly on a flat surface. Lay the other two shade pieces against the angled sides and mark the corresponding angles. Cut the last two shade pieces a little oversize.

17 The shade can now be glued together and held in place with tape. Make some full-length corner glue blocks to strengthen the joint.

18 Mark out the position for the bolts by lining up the external and top edge of the arm pieces and drawing a square. The deep mortise on the bridle joint will allow the arm to adjust beyond 90° in both directions.

19 Cut 10° angles on the ends of the blocks that hold the complete arm assembly in place. Keep one of the offcuts.

20 Use the offcut as a spacer on the shooting board to give you the 10° angle you need.

21 Mark out for the bolt hole on one of the support blocks. Note that the arm needs to be able to rotate beyond the vertical. You can accomplish this by drawing a circle using the center of the square and the distance to the corner as its radius.

22 As a precaution, you can drill a couple of holes in one of the support blocks through to the arm to insert a peg or tapered wooden nail.

23 Bolt the arm and support blocks together and attach to the base with screws. Don't glue in place until you are sure that the base is sufficiently large to prevent the lamp from tipping over when the electrical components are installed.

24 When the shade has been levelled off, attach it to the block with wooden tapered nails or dowels. Again, don't glue it in place until you have installed your electrical components.

*Your finished desk lamp will look something like this.*

# GLOSSARY

**Bandsaw** Stationary workshop machine that uses a continuous blade running along two or sometimes three wheels and through a metal worktable. Can be used for cutting curved shapes, joints, and resawing wood into smaller pieces or veneer.

**Bearing-guided bit** Router bit with an integral roller bearing that runs against the workpiece or a suitable template to produce a consistent depth of cut or matching profile.

**Bench hook** Workshop-made jig to hold wood securely when crosscutting with a hand saw.

**Bench plane** Typically a two-handled plane between No. 4 and No. 6 sizes. Different lengths and widths can be used for straightening, flattening, and smoothing wood.

**Bevel** A slope, such as the sharpening angle on a blade or a sloping edge on a piece of wood. A bevel is often used for decoration.

**Biscuit** Oval-shaped, flat, compressed-wood piece used in conjunction with a biscuit jointer. When used with water-based glue, the biscuit will swell, making a very secure joint. Available in several sizes to suit different wood thicknesses.

**Block plane** Small plane available with a low-angled blade for use on end grain and small components.

**Chamfer** Similar to a bevel but cut symmetrically to both surfaces at 45°.

**Combination square** Metal tool combining the functions of a try square, miter square, and steel rule.

**Coping saw** Small frame saw with a narrow blade for cutting curves by hand.

**Countersink bit** Conical drill bit that creates a funnel-shaped recess at the top of a drilled hole to allow the screw head to sit flush with or below the surface of the wood.

**Crosscutting** Sawing across the grain of the wood, reducing the length of a board.

**Dovetail** A friction joint consisting of spear-shaped pegs cut into the end of one component that fit into corresponding gaps cut into the second.

**Dowel** Round peg or cylindrical length of wood.

**Elevation** Drawing of an object as viewed from one side.

**End grain** The fibers at the end of a board that are exposed by crosscutting.

**Fence** Used with a power tool or machine to align the workpiece accurately in relation to the bit or blade.

**Fret saw** Small frame saw with a fine narrow blade for cutting curves by hand and gaining access to tight corners.

**Guide rail** Metal rail designed to be used with power tools such as routers and circular saws so that they will move accurately across a workpiece.

**Hardwood** Produced by deciduous trees such as oak or ash. Not always hard in the literal sense – for example, balsa is classed as a hardwood.

**Hone** To produce a finely sharpened edge using an abrasive stone after grinding.

**Kerf** The gap in the wood left by a saw blade.

**Mallet** Hammer-type tool with a wooden, or sometimes rubber, striking head. Used for driving chisels into hardwood and for knocking joints together.

**Marking gauge** A wooden gauge for marking lines parallel to the edge of a workpiece edge.

**Miter gauge** Sliding fence on a router table or table saw used for square or angled crosscutting.

**Mortise and tenon** Traditional wood joint with a rectangular peg (tenon) formed on one component and a matching socket (mortise) cut into the other.

**Pilot hole** Hole bored in wood to accommodate a screw shank but not the thread. Used to ease screw insertion and prevent wood from splitting.

**Plan view** Drawing of an object as viewed from above.

**Rabbet** A step-shaped recess cut on the edge of a workpiece. Often made to fit a corresponding tongue on a neighboring piece.

**Rasp** A metal file with coarse teeth used to shape wood.

**Ripping** Sawing parallel to the grain of the wood along the length of a board.

**Scribe** To mark a line.

**Section** Term used to describe a drawing where some components of the object are cut through.

**Shooting board** A flat board with a fence or an adjustable backstop at one end. Used to trim wood to dimension with the use of a suitable plane.

**Shoulder plane** A thin hand plane with tall flat sides that are machined square to the base of the body. Used to trim the shoulders of tenons or other joints.

**Sliding bevel** Adjustable tool used for capturing and transferring angles for cutting or alignment.

**Softwood** Wood produced by coniferous trees, such as pine.

**Spokeshave** A metal or wooden tool with a handle on either side of a blade for shaping wood. Particularly useful for creating round stock.

**Tenon saw** Small fine-toothed saw used for joint-cutting and bench work. Usually has a metal stiffening strip along the back of the blade for extra rigidity. For this reason it is also called a back saw.

**Try square** L-shaped tool designed for marking 90° angles using the workpiece edge as a reference.

**Web clamp** Used for clamping irregular shapes. It has a strap tightened with a ratcheting mechanism and can incorporate corner pieces as required.

**Wheel gauge** A metal gauge with a circular disc for marking lines parallel to a workpiece edge. A type of marking gauge.

# SUPPLIERS

The following suppliers offer the tools used in this book.

**Highland Woodworking**
www.highlandwoodworking.com
800-241-6748

**Japan Woodworker**
www.japanwoodworker.com
800-537-7820

**Rockler**
www.rockler.com
800-279-4441

**Woodcraft**
www.woodcraft.com
800-225-1153

# ABOUT THE AUTHOR

Derek Jones began his career in furniture-making as an apprentice in a restoration workshop in Brighton, England. What felt like an insufferable amount of time spent cleaning old furniture and removing layers of thick, sticky varnish was in fact time well spent. Observing the complete range of techniques used to construct everything from a breakfront bookcase to a carriage clock case was a fantastic opportunity to learn the tricks of the trade from past masters.

A course in 3D design convinced him to switch his focus to the design and making of custom furniture and joinery. In 2009, he became the Editor of *Furniture & Cabinetmaking* magazine, and frequently delves into his past experiences to evoke the same fascination with objects and the making process with new practitioners of the craft.

"It's great to be working with the accumulated knowledge of years of experience, but nothing compares to the excitement and enthusiasm when you're desperate to learn a new skill," says Derek.

# INDEX

Project names in *italics*



---


To order a book, or to request a catalog, contact:
The Taunton Press, Inc.
63 South Main Street, P.O. Box 5506,Newtown, CT 06470-5506
Tel (800) 888-8286
www.taunton.com